C0-ARE-730

ME, MYSELF, & I

ME, MYSELF, & I

Everywoman's Journey to Her Self

Ann
Schoonmaker

Harper & Row, Publishers
New York, Hagerstown, San Francisco, London

ME, MYSELF, AND I. Copyright © 1977 by Ann Schoonmaker. All rights reserved. Printed in the United States of America. No part of this book may be used or reproduced in any manner whatsoever without written permission except in the case of brief quotations embodied in critical articles and reviews. For information address Harper & Row, Publishers, Inc., 10 East 53rd Street, New York, N.Y. 10022. Published simultaneously in Canada by Fitzhenry & Whiteside Limited, Toronto.

FIRST EDITION

Designed by Janice Stern

ISBN: 0–06–067120–3
LC: 76–62958

The world of humanity is possessed by two wings—
the male and the female. So long as these two wings are not
equivalent in strength the bird will not fly. Until
womankind reaches the same degree as man, until she
enjoys the same arena of activity, extraordinary attainment for humanity will not be realized; humanity can not
wing its way to heights of real attainment.

—'Abdu'l-Bahá
The Promulgation of Universal Peace[1]

Contents

PREFACE

Right now the status of the women's movement in this country leaves me feeling there's a tremendous amount of confusion and lost energy because we don't seem to have an overview. A lot of women talk about different points of view which are related to their stages of personal growth and development, but nobody's spelled out in simple terms just what stages might lead a woman toward personal liberation. Much of the time women in one stage of growth blame women who aren't at that same stage. They seem unwilling to acknowledge the right and responsibility of others to be where they are. Nobody's asking, Just what happens in the process of consciousness raising that facilitates new growth and awareness? What specific tasks must we each face?

This book is a sort of rough sketch of the various growth stages that may occur within the developmental process in women. It's an overview, not a specific map of any particular task, such as learning how to be assertive or more intimate. It's drawn from my own experiences as well as from those of friends and other women with whom I've worked as a counselor.

I believe each of us has two tasks: to find out who we are and to find out who we are not. The first task involves establishing a personal form of identity. It includes, but is more than, our roles in life, our relationships, and our physical being. In this slow inner process we sort ourselves out from other people so that we can become whole, individual, and separate. Then we build new relationships on that basis. The second task involves finding meaning and purpose in life, faith in something beyond us—call it religion, philosophy, or what you will.

In the process of writing this book and in living through the experiences which have contributed to it, I stand indebted to many friends, teachers, therapists, and colleagues. I would like to acknowledge these relationships and the positive input these persons have made in my life and hence to this book. But I take responsibility for the way I've put it together—both my life and the book—as well as the mistakes and difficulties along the way.

So thank you especially to friends Jean Yale Boyd, Jane Yale Rush, Helen Mallon, Joan Taylor, Gerry Piorkowski, Pat Finley; teachers Nelle Morton, Carl Michalson, Sam Banks, Tom Oden, Nelson Thayer, Bard Thompson, Thelma Dixon-Murphy; therapists Jim Ranck, Reuben Blanck, David Hart, Philip Zabriskie; colleagues Larry Kesner, Roger Plantikow, Garry Rea-Airth.

Beyond these special people I want to thank the members of my family who have had to live with my working and writing, especially my youngest daughter, Laura, for her patient waiting "until I finish this chapter . . ." I thank two other special persons, my editor Marie Cantlon, who had faith in this book from its earliest outlines, and copy editor Pat Pratt, who pruned and clarified the text so it made more sense.

ANN SCHOONMAKER
Summit, New Jersey
September 1976

INTRODUCTION

The Inner Task
of Women's Liberation

When we go down a road for the first time, everything seems new. There's more to see than we can look at. About all we can do is get from point A to point B without missing a turn. On a second trip, we begin to recognize certain landmarks—waterfalls, bridges, steep hills, interesting buildings like bubble houses, strange old trees, beautiful gardens. After four or five times down the same road, the way begins to seem familiar. We can even begin to tell other people how to get there.

The trip through life is something like that. We set out on a long, long trip without a roadmap to tell us where to go or what the highways are like. It's as though we set out to cross the continent of North America from the Atlantic to the Pacific without any notion of where or how to go except to follow the sun from east to west.

Only recently have scientists begun to study the total growth and development of persons from birth to death. For years the main emphasis has been on the stages children grow through and their various ups and downs. Books by Drs. Spock, Gesell, and Ilg have helped us understand children's growth but not our own. Most books about adult life focus on what seems to be wrong and how to get "better." Others deal with specific tasks, such as how to be more assertive or more intimate. We can't find much about the normal, natural stages of life and how to recognize where we've gotten stuck.

As women, our psychological growth still remains pretty much a mystery. We know we share certain physical experiences as we pass through stages of bodily growth. For example, in puberty our breasts and hips grow and we have our first menstrual periods. But intercourse, pregnancy, childbirth, and child raising present opportunities for personal choice. We pass through common stages in personal growth and development; yet despite all the talk about "consciousness raising," nobody's spelled out what that process involves. It's time to sketch out at least a rough map illustrating our various stages of development as women so that we can share and compare our experiences in light of common knowledge.

Why bother? Because the leading edge of the women's movement is right where each woman is in her growth and development. Not enough has been said about the fact that *all true liberation comes from the inside.* The more we study the link between the inner and outer tasks of the women's movement, the more we realize that we can't move any faster on the social, economic, and legal front than we do on the inner, personal front. We can change outer conditions only in direct relationship to inner attitudes women have about themselves and the way they value themselves and others. Women who ignore this fact find themselves at one stage of growth fighting needlessly against women in other stages. They struggle to achieve personal equality by sacrificing all the human values they repressed along with the Feminine. In truth, we are all involved together, moving along similar paths at different rates of speed. Trying to move too fast means that we lose sight of one another along the way. Certainly there have been many economic and legal injustices against women as human beings which must be changed, but these evils will be remedied when we become ready as individuals. Women who are not ready needn't have to fight women who are.

What women need most of all is emotional liberation from the social patterns and spells that have limited our personal growth and kept us from establishing personal identities. This sort of growth has nothing to do with IQ or book learning or with being married, single, mothers, career women, young, or old. It occurs during a long process in which we establish specific ego-strengths and work through particular conflicts.

In one respect this means we move away from the dependence of early childhood toward independence and autonomy, away from being passive toward being active and able to take initiative. We move away from role playing and narcissistic self-love which ignore other persons into a new way of honoring others' integrity as well as our own. We move from the stage in which we may drift along unconsciously as victims of our own emotional blocks to a stage in which we are able to make choices and decisions based upon knowing our real alternatives. This involves being able to take concrete, creative action in the world instead of just talking or thinking about it.

But this process of change is more than just moving from one point to another. It's like the metamorphosis of caterpillar to butterfly because it involves a shift within our inner attitudes about how we view life. It means learning that we have personal freedom to choose our inner responses regardless of the situation. It means consciously realizing that freedom. We can choose to become despairing and bitter, despondent and depressed, resentful and self-destructive; or we can channel our energies into taking personal responsibility for our lives and working through the possible alternatives. The important thing is first to get in touch with our creative centers and then begin working constructively together at opening doors to change. If we don't, we get caught in various mix-ups—waiting for others to see what's wrong, wondering why nobody's doing anything. Needs we see clearly ourselves, we can begin working on. We can flex our emotional and spiritual muscles and act for ourselves.

But movement and change don't come easily. The end result sounds good, but the process is painful and difficult. It means living through a mixture of feelings—fear, anger, frustration, loneliness, guilt, and shame—and living through periods of loss and abandonment, as well as getting confused and being tired. It means stretching out, risking, reaching past every limit we've ever known. It means stepping forward into a blank unknown, falling down flat, and then picking ourselves up and starting over again.

To admit that the process of growth and development is painful and messy and often just plain hard work may not seem much incentive for anyone to begin the journey, but most of us get pushed into the process before we know it. Often we don't know we're involved until we begin hurting. Then our goal is to relieve the pain any way we can. We're willing to look closer at ourselves to see what we've been doing to get boxed in. Sometimes everything has been going along great, and then suddenly everything falls apart.

This may apply to you. Perhaps you have been hurting but have been unable to put your finger on just what is bothering you. You may feel frustrated, bored, depressed, suffocated, angry, or desperate. These feelings may be the clues that something is stirring in you, something that needs and wants to grow. Sometimes it seems safer to ignore those feelings and stay where we are, but we all have an innate spirit of growth that cannot be denied without peril to ourselves and to others.

When we deny needs for growth, we put our needs for fulfillment upon other people. We become—or more truthfully, we stay—dependent puppets, relying on someone else to pull the strings. If we don't continue to grow throughout our lives, we start dying psychologically. It can be scary to walk by ourselves. The future may seem blank or foggy. The risk of change is often more threatening than the pain of staying where we are, but the future can also be exciting: Somewhere in our background lurks the spiritual potential not only to walk but to run, skip, dance—and eventually to fly!

For me, all the times of hurting—loss, frustration, despair—turned out to be thresholds into new developmental stages. When I first began looking back, my life seemed to be a series of ups and downs, zigzags back and forth, forward three steps and backward two. During the highs I risked new experiences, set new goals, and worked toward them. I ventured into territory outside my old patterns; I found new ways to stand my ground and speak out for myself.

During the lows I seemed to regress; I didn't know who I was, and I didn't care. At times my whole world closed in; I couldn't make any sense out of what was happening, and I felt especially vulnerable and dependent. Most of those times I felt either guilty or inadequate. I had to fight some inner bondage that kept me back; whenever my growing spirit tried to break free, I blocked myself with feelings of guilt, shame, anxiety, and inadequacy. I needed new ways to relate both to myself and to others. I needed to reown the pieces of myself I had disowned along the path of my life.

Since I began seeing a pattern in my highs and lows, I've met other women who have been fighting the same inner bondage. In talking with them and comparing notes, I discovered that we have moved through the same conflicts. It's as though we've been down the same road at different times, sharing the same frustrations, fears, and lonely feelings as we struggled separately to find our way.

FOUR STAGES

In this book I describe four stages of growth and development for women, an overview of the process, including conflicts and tasks. In away it's like a huge map of North America, showing the typical features like mountains, rivers, and plains. I hope this map will provide enough coordinates for you to locate yourself and others. Later on you may want to read other books, much as you would turn to more detailed maps of Illinois or Chicago if you were in that location and wanted specific information. In the bibliography I suggest a few of many books you can use for that purpose.

The four main sections present the different growth stages as a sort of "psychogeography." You can think of each stage as one particular state of mind or level of consciousness. Each stage represents not only the way we behave but the way we see ourselves and relate to others. During each stage we must work through particular tasks and conflicts. While we are in one stage, we generally have no awareness of the next.

When we have done fully the work of each stage and grown into it completely, then it's time to move on to the next—a major shift in our development. "Moving on" is often difficult and painful, for it involves risk and giving up earlier ways of being. But if we don't move on, then the completed stage becomes a "cage," and we remain fixated, frustrated, and blocked. Our spirit feels restricted whether we admit it or not.

As we move through the first three stages—*Me, Myself,* and *I*—we develop various ego-strengths and form our personal identity.

Me

As infants we begin in the Me stage. During growth periods we can be thrown back into this stage because our egos cannot handle new conflicts. Powerful emotional forces triggered by deep psychological needs can overwhelm us so that we lose track of ourselves. For example, romantic love pulls couples into such close relationships that it's hard to tell one mate from the other. Mothers often become so identified with their children that they possess no individuality of their own.

There are five basic characteristics of the Me stage:

1. The woman is unconscious of both herself and others; she is often caught in repetitive patterns from which she cannot escape.
2. She has no personal identity but derives identity vicariously from some physical-emotional relationship. For example, she may see herself as Harry's daughter, Sam's wife, Bill's secretary, or Gladys's mother.
3. She is completely dependent upon and overidentifies with important others; she assumes she knows what they are thinking and feeling without question and is hurt if they do not know what she wants without asking.
4. She has a basic conflict between feelings of depression and anxiety on one side and her fears of separation, loneliness, and the unknown future on the other.
5. Her basic task is to develop sufficient trust in her self as good and entitled to personal growth—to feel OK and equal to everyone else.

Myself

In the Myself stage we begin to recognize our selfhood but are still caught between being passive and finding ourselves. In this in-between stage we gradually separate from others and begin to establish our uniqueness. Ideally this stage occurs during physiological adolescence when children separate from parents and find patterns of living in the world based upon their own choices. Often, however, women miss out on this stage. They go from being dependent upon their parents to being dependent upon their husbands or their bosses. They continue to need someone to contain them so that they need not grow—or because they have not grown. We never completely outgrow the Me part of ourselves but continue to have natural dependency needs all our lives. In the Myself stage we develop the capacity to choose between times we can allow ourselves to be passive, dependent, and vulnerable and times when we can be independent and active on behalf of ourselves. Most books about becoming an assertive woman fall into this category of working through the Myself stage.

The five basic characteristics of this stage are:

1. This period of transition is marked by a woman's emerging awareness of herself as a separate person.
2. She begins to move gradually toward developing her personal identity.
3. She begins a process of separation and different-iation from the important people in her life, still loving and relating to them but learning to be her own self without clinging dependently to them.
4. Her basic conflict is between feelings of emptiness, frustration, boredom, and a sense of drifting along through life and fear of asserting herself. She feels ashamed of herself and guilty if she is too different from anyone else.
5. Her basic task is to find her own space and ground in relation to others so that she can begin to develop personal capabilities and take responsibility for her decisions and actions.

I

The I stage requires our becoming more fully aware and conscious of our selfhood in an active, independent, resourceful, and responsible way. In this stage, for the first time we begin to be competent at whatever life work we have chosen. This means that a woman running a home can be just as fully conscious and resourceful as a woman who terms herself a career person. The I stage is the taking-charge stage. We have to work through new tasks in interpersonal relationships as well as unresolved conflicts from the Me and Myself stages. It's easy to be thrown backward, to feel inadequate or guilty.

The five basic characteristics of the I stage are:

1. The woman takes conscious responsibility for herself and her actions.
2. She has established herself as a person, beyond whatever outer social identity she may have in relation to someone else.
3. She is able to care and share with others freely without being over-whelmed by them or dominating them. She can be alone without over-whelming feelings of loneliness.
4. Her basic conflicts are between feelings of anger and injustice, when she is ignored as a person, and her fears of competing with others, taking authority, and being successful.
5. Her basic tasks are to own herself completely, to become able to take initiative, and to become competent in some form of work.

I/Thou

After we have moved through the first three stages and find our-selves mostly in the I state of mind, we have established what psy-chologists would term *ego identity.* The English language is difficult sometimes, especially when it comes to that word *ego.* When I use it, I mean that inner core of awareness that enables us to deal consciously with conflicts and choose between various courses of action. We all need egos, but we don't need to be egotistical.

During the fourth stage, however, a curious thing happens. Just as we establish a sense of ego identity, our next task is to relinquish the centrality of our ego and admit to our consciousness a new sense of the mysterious. This is the I/Thou stage, a phrase first coined by the philosopher Martin Buber to describe a special realm of the spirit and the soul which is linked with God or the transcendent. We do not move into this stage by conscious choice. Generally we are thrown into it against our will because we have come face-to-face with our personal limits. This is a time of death and rebirth, a time when our egos give way to what has been termed the deeper Self. In this stage we finally have to recognize the mystery of life and face its deeper meaning. Often we must pass through the valley of the shadow of death before we begin to sense that our lives stand under a higher authority which the ordinary world cannot comprehend.

The five basic characteristics of this stage are:

1. Recognizing the power of the creative unconscious and that our conscious minds have limits.
2. Accepting personal, human limitations as we stand before the mystery of life.
3. Learning to share a true intimacy with others in which our selves honor and value another equally before God, despite whatever outward differences may appear to separate us. We then can celebrate our differences instead of ignoring them or fighting over them.
4. The basic conflict during this period is a loss of faith and despair, with a sense of meaninglessness, and a search for the deeper meaning of life so that we have new faith and purpose.
5. The basic task during this period is to accept all the pieces of ourselves we may have disowned earlier and to face the unknown with wholeness and integrity.

OF LISTS AND LIVES

In describing the four stages, I've given objective, condensed lists of the characteristics in each. Such lists can be helpful for a quick overview of the territory, but they fail to provide the personal emotional aspects which bring the stages alive. Lists are sterile and impersonal and cannot convey how life unfolds in real people. To do this we need images of women in each stage, images with which you can identify or use to identify others. Images are important to me, for they can often condense in one key word a whole complex personality. If I say *Scarlett O'Hara,* you get an immediate conception of how life unfolded for one woman through various stages of her life. Similarly I might use *Lucy* (of the television series "I Love Lucy"), *Edith Bunker* (of "All in the Family"), or *Pepper* (of "Policewoman") to suggest three different images of contemporary women which match up pretty well with the stages of Me, Myself, and I.

In order to bring each stage alive, I will use images both from mass media and from various personal experiences. The individuals I describe are a composite of real women I've known—any resemblance to someone you know is purely accidental.

FOUR STAGES IN A WOMAN'S GROWTH AND DEVELOPMENT

Ann Schoonmaker ©

STAGE	ME	MYSELF	I	I/THOU
Level of Consciousness	Unconscious	Beginning awareness of self	Conscious responsibility for self	Recognition of creative unconscious
Type of Identity	None of own; derived from others	Gradual development of own	Personal identity established	Recognition of human limitations
Relationships with Others	Dependent; identify other as self	Beginning of separation; difference felt	Caring, sharing without getting lost in other	True intimacy; honor, value other as self though different
Common Feelings	Anxiety, depression	Emptiness, frustration, boredom, drifting	Anger, sense of injustice, tension	Loss of faith; despair
Common Fears	Separation, loneliness, the unknown	Shame and guilt over self-assertion	Competition, taking authority, success	Meaninglessness
Developmental Tasks	Basic trust in own self; personal worth	Finding one's own space and ground	Taking initiative, being competent	Accepting lost parts of self and the unknown

The Me State
of Mind

The Me stage is a normal period in everyone's life and remains part of us throughout life. As infants, our survival depends on others' love and care. We continue to need warmth, caring, and affection, but as we grow older, we normally outgrow the Me stage of total dependence on others for our needs. During adolescence we begin to establish a sense of identity as persons in our own right.

Unfortunately, many women never grow out of the Me stage. They remain trapped in it by their own unconscious needs and by social patterns they do not have enough personal strength to resist. In a way, they start off on the pathway through life but get stuck somewhere along the line. They remain basically passive, dependent, and unconscious.

I've given the name *Matilda* to a generalized description of the woman who remains in this stage. I will use several other images to illustrate the different ways women can become trapped in the Me stage and will discuss some magical spells that keep these women in bondage, unable to break free by themselves. Finally we'll take a look at the process of spell breaking which can lead these women into the next stage of beginning to find themselves.

CHAPTER 1

Me and Matilda

EVERYTHING HAPPENS TO ME!

Matilda personifies the Me woman. Everything happens *to* her—good things, bad things, in-between things. She never seems to take responsibility for herself. Life just happens to her—jobs, parties, accidents, slips of the tongue, slips on the ice, slips up, slips down. You name it and she's had it—and she's been had in turn. She's apt to assume the victim's role every time. She's the picture of innocence and naivete, and her sympathetic heart bleeds for everyone and everybody—except herself. She's endearing, charming, the perennial "girl" wandering unconsciously through life, sort of like Alice in Wonderland.

I know Matilda well because I've been her, and she is still a part of my Me-ness. I lived in that state of mind for many years, completely unconscious of who I was or what life was all about, caught in various spells I took for granted. I've spent a lot of time working out of that stage, but I know I can easily slip back under stress and strain. Being Matilda can be a happy time, as long as it lasts, for she coasts along, living vicariously through someone else—husband, child, supervisor, boss. Unfortunately, situations change, and the "days of wine and roses" fade.

You've probably known lots of Matildas and can detect the times you are like her, just as I can. The biggest clue to Matilda is that her center is outside herself. She is perennially searching for something

15

external to explain what life is all about; she's keen on horoscopes, tea leaves, and even the *I Ching* which she uses in a magical way to slip past reality. Anything she can find to explain what has "happened" to her is great. Without any question or reserve, she accepts anybody who'll give her advice on how to run her life.

As "innocent" victim, she's the ideal spectator, passively watching others from the sidelines. Always outside the action, she cheers her kids on at a ball game or in a swimming race. In the office, she works triple overtime, often without pay, just so her boss will have all the necessary papers for his big presentation. Her life depends on moments when someone important to her achieves something for her vicariously, but all those accomplishments come secondhand. She never quite dares risk herself or her own capabilities.

Matilda's also a great one for knowing everything about the lives of other people and for criticizing how the other person is doing a job. Nothing is ever quite good enough. She sees things ideally and romantically, but she never gets out on the front line herself. She's happy to work away in the background, taking orders, and doing everything she can to make someone else's project a success. She's the ideal vice-president, the adoring little wife, the irreplaceable office-wife. She's the passive slave to anyone who'll be her master or mistress.

Whether she's ten, twenty, forty, or fifty years old, Matilda's a darling little girl. She's Sleeping Beauty, Little Red Riding Hood, Little Miss Muffet, and Mistress Mary all rolled into one. She's just not in touch with the real world, or at least her part of it. She never quite hears what others are really talking about and interrupts with anything that might get attention.

On the surface she's good and perfect—so perfect you suspect there's nothing beneath the surface. Flat and two-dimensional, she performs the life-scripts other people write for her. To top it off, she's like the woman in the joke who, after her husband says, "The trouble with women in business is that they always take things personally," answers sweetly, "But *I* never do!"

VARIATIONS ON A THEME

Matildas come in various sizes and shapes, but they have one common characteristic—things happen to them. I know Matilda intimately through my personal pilgrimage, via experiences friends have shared, and from my work as a counselor. Matildas eagerly await a fairy godmother to solve their problems, patch up their lives, and send them back into the world to go on living in the same old way. They have no idea that they need to change—inside.

Mona Brown was a Matilda. Once upon a time she worked in an office. Then Prince Charming came along. They married and had three children, but now nothing in her life was going right. Nobody could do anything to please her. Her husband wouldn't take her shopping at nights to the big suburban malls she loved to explore. She couldn't drive and had never even considered learning. Her children wouldn't do their chores, nor would they speak respectfully to her. She spent most of the day up in her bedroom, watching television and eating. Underneath she hated everybody, but most of all she hated herself. She didn't understand that each day presents an opportunity to make choices that would change the pattern of her life. She was content to depend on somebody else for everything and then be totally miserable because "they" wouldn't take care of her the way she expected. It seemed to me she had never even learned to toddle emotionally. Spiritually, she was a stillborn child.

Marcia Smith was a lovely, well-educated woman whose husband had left for another woman years before, leaving her to manage with one little boy. She had become a completely adoring mother, worshiping at the shrine of her son. But in adolescence he turned into someone she could barely recognize. He fought with her and against her constantly. Finally he ran away to find a life of his own. Marcia blamed everybody else for her problems. Nothing had ever been her fault. If only she could turn back the clock to her childhood when she had been daddy's favorite little girl and had everything she wanted. Now she waited passively for me to fix up her life. Should she risk another marriage? Would this new man be able to treat her like daddy had?

Maybelle Jones no longer loved her husband but suspected he was cheating behind her back. (He was.) What would she do without him now that her children were gone? Marianne Johnson's desperate ex-husband told me, just after he escaped from her clutches, that he'd felt like he was being choked to death by an octopus whenever he was with her. She was always clinging to him—which she admitted, because "without him, she'd die." Miriam Thompson was in love, but her mother didn't approve. "How could she decide between her mother and her lover?" Maxine Black had been a brilliant, gifted musician before she married and had kids. Now she was driving both herself and her husband to drink. Their children had grown up, and she hadn't been able to find herself or an outlet for her energies.

These Matildas represent women at a turning point in their lives. Those who came to me for counseling wanted advice on how to get out of their cages or on how to redecorate the only way of life they'd ever known. Even if I'd been able to open their cage doors, it wouldn't have done any good. Each was an unhatched chicken who would need to be warmed a long time before she gained enough strength to peck her way out of the shell.

Matilda has never had the opportunity to exercise her muscle of selfhood. She's been carried along or pushed, like a baby in a carriage. She's never been allowed down on the ground so that she might reach out and stretch for something she saw and wanted.

Matilda is seductive. She can beguile someone into wanting to change her and mold her, to offer her courses and give her books containing recipes for what's been missing in her life. Matilda's dependency can be charming, just like that of a small child. She can manage beautifully to manipulate anyone who enjoys being needed that way.

Because Matilda never learned to crawl or walk by herself emotionally, she requires others to fill her empty center. She pulls them into her vacuum of meaning and purpose—husband, child, pet or pet cause, or employer. By remaining centered on another, she perpetuates her dependency. The empty nest problem, which many women experience during menopause and/or when their children leave home, is the best example of how long women can live without having to find them-*selves.* One minister told me sadly that many women never "came into their own and blossomed" until the death of their husbands.

Paradoxically, Matilda is also a me-first person. She forces others to take care of her. Matilda clings until others realize they have been manipulated by her vulnerability; then they rebel and walk out. And Matilda wonders what happened *to her.* Everything is somebody else's fault. Matilda can be the most "self-ish" person there is because she never takes responsibility for herself.

On the other hand, Matilda is also the most-trapped woman; she is powerless to help herself. It would be easy to say that all Matildas are superficial, immature, and shallow human beings, but the catch is, our society has encouraged and reinforced this level of existence for millions of women. Just as golf courses have sand traps, our society has emotional traps into which women fall as easily as golf balls— especially if their early childhood experience didn't give them an opportunity to grow as persons.

ME-NESS IN GENERAL

The Matilda stage is a continuation of the ground level in human development. As infants, we all begin with the Me stage. We are completely unconscious of self and are totally dependent on others for survival. Psychologists say that the mother and her newborn baby initially exist in a close unity known as *symbiosis.* The baby has no consciousness of itself, and the mother instinctively tunes in to the baby's needs. The mother's faith that life is good and worth living results in the baby's learning to trust in life and in itself. The mother's ego serves as a container within which the baby's self begins to grow.

This Me stage is also the first phase in the social development of human groups. All over the world thousands of groups of people still live on this level. It is normal and natural for everyone in such a group to remain unconscious of themselves and dependent upon others for survival. Anthropologists term this stage *participation mystique,* when everyone in the group is mysteriously one with everyone else.

This phase of life then is completely normal for infants and for members of social groups in undeveloped countries. We have problems in our country because we've thrown together all kinds of groups and failed to recognize that growing up in a complicated society like ours means that children need help in developing self-reliance and responsibility for survival. Children grow out of the Me stage at different rates and begin to find themselves as persons in different ways—always at their own pace. Growing out of this stage cannot be forced. It is first a matter of individual readiness and inner maturation and second of expectations and support from other people. We don't beat babies for not beginning to walk when we want them to; neither can we beat late-blooming Matildas.

Growing out of the Me stage is now theoretically possible for every person on this planet. The problem comes when such growth is not encouraged or is blocked, as it is in the United States for many women, or when it is expected prematurely without adequate developmental support. It is tragic that millions starve to death from physical hunger because we have not yet made it a priority to find ways to feed everyone. It is even more tragic that millions die emotionally and spiritually. They are starved psychologically, and their growth has been blunted. When you see pictures of vacant, empty faces of women trapped in poverty, misery, ignorance, and stillbornness, perhaps you grieve as I do.

Perhaps you also are angry and want to do something about it. I am enraged over the binding of women's hearts, souls, and minds today just as I was horrified over the binding of little girls' feet in Oriental countries years ago. It is one thing for this to happen in undeveloped countries where good nutrition and education have not been possible, but it is blatantly intolerable that it happens in a country dedicated on paper to the equal rights of all to life, liberty, and the pursuit of happiness.

But anger by itself does not provide the means for social change.

What we need is a means for recognizing the manner in which women have been unconsciously bound and trapped. Then we can work together at changing mental attitudes and set new standards for what will be considered socially acceptable. We no longer accept as normal a situation in which babies develop rickets because they lack vitamin D and calcium in whole milk. We no longer accept beriberi or scurvy as natural diseases. We know they are caused by lack of wholesome natural foods.

Someday we will no longer accept little girls being allowed to grow into physical maturity while remaining undeveloped emotionally. In the past we have accepted all too easily women's lack of self-esteem as well as their inability to achieve selfhood. Unfortunately the incapacity of women to achieve independence and autonomy has been taken for granted too long. Women still suffer from needless shame and guilt when they begin to demonstrate personal initiative.

Right now we are living in an "in-between" time. It is still too acceptable for parents to ignore their daughters and take it for granted that all they will ever do is get through school and marry. Really good education for sons has been a priority in many families; daughters could manage without it. The idea is innovative that young girls need a good education so they can better educate the young children entrusted to their care. We have had few models for what women might achieve beyond family life. Marilyn Monroe and Judy Garland are tragic examples of expectations and limitations our society has imposed upon women. Madame Curie, Amelia Earhart, and Eleanor Roosevelt are exceptional illustrations of how women can be different.

And women have bought into these social expectations even when they have been educated and given every advantage to do otherwise. They have done so partly because they were ignorant of alternatives and partly because our society lacks the means to recognize where women are and what might be blocking or trapping them. Unfortunately we not only fail to communicate, but we fail in knowing what to communicate.

CHAPTER 2

Spellbound

Most Matildas are spellbound, or blocked in their emotional development. Psychologists are just beginning to discover what causes this. We are learning to recognize the games we play, the unconscious scripts we live out, and how we present ourselves in a variety of superficial roles. I prefer to call any pattern we get locked into so that we cannot grow by an old-fashioned term: *spell,* a word common in fairy tales and myths. The dictionary gives three meanings for *spell* which fit together nicely to describe what I mean: (1) a "period of enchantment" which results from some sort of "irresistible influence or fascination"; (2) a specific period of time, as in "come in and bide a spell"; and (3) when we *spell* out something, we explain it so clearly and carefully that the meaning is unmistakable.

Women are caught in such spells, first of all, because they are often irresistibly influenced by outside forces. Even though there can be unique individual spells, most women are caught in spells cast by their social group, and they find it impossible to break out alone. They are trapped within a larger system and need outside help to escape. For example, a romantic spell can carry a woman away just as an undertow can carry away even the strongest swimmer.

Our society casts other spells such as the perfect hero and the good child. We have taken these spells for granted for so long that we don't even question them. They are an accepted part of our cultural reality. In order to break their charm and fascination, we have to understand how they work.

A spell results when a normal, essential activity in human growth is distorted. Natural developmental crises occur at predictable stages in the human life-cycle—birth, puberty, mating, and aging, for example. During these crises natural emotions become intense. If we are developmentally unprepared to work through the crisis or if the natural emotion is so powerful our reason cannot cope, we may be overwhelmed by the trauma of the event. In other words, the growth process is distorted, and the person's emotional maturation may be frozen into that distorted form, that is, a spell.

Normally our social group provides certain "rites of passage" to celebrate major life developments. Friends and relatives gather around, providing a sense of coherence and meaning as we pass through major changes. Baptism, confirmation, wedding ceremonies, and funerals are rituals in which social groups provide necessary support according to various traditions.

Moreover, well-known stories, myths, dramatize the aspects of a crisis in a way that helps us identify with persons going through it. The names of these characters serve as key words to suggest the complete story. Freud used the story of Oedipus to describe what happens when a son is unable to break free of a fixation on his mother. Yet no one has ever really considered Jocasta, Oedipus' mother, as an example of what happens when a mother winds up living through her son.

We can use famous stories to illustrate the various spells in which women have become trapped. The heroines represent situations that we need to recognize as potential sources of enchantment and fascination. These spells involve normal growth periods in a woman's life—childhood, the natural desire for a mate and children. Problems arise when natural crises are distorted or prolonged and we fail to move out of one stage into the next.

In the spells described below we will see the normal, natural need which triggers the crisis situation during a particular growth period, the significant persons involved, and how the situation gets distorted or twisted because of unfulfilled individual and social expectations. Because growth is a lifelong process, we can observe spells from early childhood, shifting and changing over the years, as well as the development of new varieties.

SPELLS FROM EARLY CHILDHOOD

Period of Crisis: Early childhood and elementary school.

Normal Need: Loving parents who provide healthy models and give children an opportunity to grow normally and naturally into relationships in the outside world.

Normal Pattern of Growth: Child identifies with parent of the same sex in such a way as to be free to find his or her own variation in later life.

Distortions or Spells: Mistrusting parent of same sex; clinging to parent of opposite sex; growth blockages in one aspect of life (physical, emotional, mental).

Images: Dorothy and the characters in the *Wonderful Wizard of Oz,* Little Red Riding Hood, Sleeping Beauty, Barbie Doll, Pookie Adams in the *Sterile Cuckoo.*

On my kitchen window sill just above the sink are four small cast-pewter figures flanked by two gigantic philodendrons: Dorothy, the Scarecrow, the Tin Woodman, and the Cowardly Lion. By squinting just a little and using a great deal of imagination, I can create the illusion that these little people have just reached the scary forest along the yellow brick road.

I have been fascinated by the story of Dorothy for many years. In fifth grade I was delighted to discover that one of my girl friends had most of the Oz books and that she would loan them to me. I remember seeing the Judy Garland movie when it was first shown and wistfully singing "Somewhere over the Rainbow" day after day as I walked home from school. I was really pleased when television began showing the movie as a regular yearly treat, for I was as eager as my children see it.

It wasn't until recently, however, that I realized that Dorothy's

story has been my life story in a special way. Once I began to understand Dorothy's story for myself, I became convinced that she holds
the key for many women still locked in the Me stage, women who are
wandering, lost, and alone in their private lands of Oz and who are
unable to find the way home. Of course, L. Frank Baum (the man who
wrote the Oz stories) certainly didn't write the *Wonderful Wizard of
Oz* for that purpose, but sometimes artists provide images which so
illuminate our own realities that we can use the collective image as
a roadmap in our own life journey.

This story illustrates the chief difficulty many women have. We
women (like Dorothy) have believed that the all-powerful male (the
Wizard) will solve our problems. We have granted him magical powers; yet our actual problem lies within ourselves. As Dorothy did, we
must deal with the feminine aspects of our nature—Glinda, the good
Witch of the South, and the wicked Witch of the West. We have the
inner power to achieve our goals, but we have mistakenly looked
outside ourselves to the magical Wizard.

Baum also unconsciously provided a great deal of insight into
problems children can have in their relationship to parental figures.
When Baum wrote (the late nineteenth century), little was known
about how children perceive reality. We are now aware that children
cannot tolerate a situation in which their parents are unable to meet
their basic needs. They cannot face a realization that their parents are
"bad," and so they become unconsciously crippled in various ways.
Like the Tin Woodman who dared not cry, they can become emotionally incapacitated. They can fail to develop their intellectual capacities
like the Scarecrow, or they can lose their courage and willpower like
the Cowardly Lion.

A woman whose parents were inadequate may develop a split
within herself. She becomes the "bad" one and is dependent on outside authority persons to be the "good" ones who will save and
nurture her while she works at trying to become "good" herself. She
can turn herself into a "bad me" searching endlessly for the nurturing
love which will make up for the inadequate loving her parents could
not provide.

The character of Pookie Adams, which John Nichols created in the *Sterile Cuckoo,* was brilliantly portrayed by Liza Minnelli in Alvin Sargent's movie of the same name. Pookie clung to her boyfriend Jerry Payne in a crazy, wonderful way with the desperation many women feel when they have not been able to establish the necessary early tie with their mothers. The scene in the graveyard, where Pookie lies down and plays dead, demonstrated a stillborn, wistful ambivalence between life and death.

If the mother really has been a "bad" or "devouring" type, other splits can occur in the way a person perceives others, especially women. They are seen as either totally good, like the good Witch of the South, or totally bad, like the wicked Witch of the West. We see this split in "Hansel and Gretel" and "Little Red Riding Hood." The bad witch in the woods fed Hansel only to fatten him up for eating. Little Red Riding Hood was eaten by the wolf—the devouring bad-witch side of her grandmother. She had to be rescued by the good woodsman, once again the image of the good father versus the bad mother.

In other stories spells are cast by fairies whose evil side is triggered by having been ignored. Briar-Rose, the Sleeping Beauty, was placed under a curse by the one fairy godmother who had not been included in her christening party. At puberty the princess pricked her finger on a spindle and fell into a deep sleep from which only the kiss of the prince could rescue her.

Stories like these can be read on many levels, but in each, a special male hero must rescue the damsel in distress. Today in real life many Sleeping Beauties are cast in the spell-like form of Barbie Doll. Incredibly beautiful but out of contact with their inner beauty, they are unapproachable by any man. Sleeping their way through shallow lives, they are untouched by deeper emotions or their sexuality. Women who have been put into psychological sleep as children are especially vulnerable to the mystical spell of romance, never realizing that it is their inner prince who must rescue them, not a dream projected onto some idealized man.

SPELLS RELATED TO IDENTITY AND ROMANCE IN
ADOLESCENCE

Normal Need: To develop a sense of identity which enables one to be intimate in an emotional and physical relationship with a partner of the opposite sex and to find a work pattern for personal skills and talents.

Normal Pattern of Growth: Courtship and marriage which encourage continuing growth in each partner and various forms of creative activity.

Distortion or Spell: Incompleted personal identity; parts of the self are projected onto the partner of the opposite sex; various immature relationships which lead to cyclical divorce and remarriage.

Several spells begin around the need within each of us to find a partner of the opposite sex and to establish a warm, loving relationship. If our normal growth has been blocked, we seek a partner who will fulfill our undeveloped potential.

The first of these spells, and the deadliest, I call the Venus Trap. This spell polarizes male and female into stereotypes and results in the mystique of romantic love. For centuries men in the Western world have marveled over the power of Venus and love to inspire them or lead them astray from their true callings. But, for centuries, no one has questioned the other half of the bargain. What about the even greater power of Venus to beguile or entrap women into playing one of her roles? In a tragic way, the plant called Venus's-flytrap illustrates the way young girls can be caught in the middle of adolescence by falling in love, marrying, and bearing children.

Romantic love appears to be such a simple, wonderful thing (everybody loves a lover, so they say), and so is Venus's-flytrap just a simple little plant. It only grows about one foot high, with clusters of small white flowers rising beside pairs of strange leaves, but these leaves have a remarkable capacity to trap insects. Each leaf is divided into two halves which have three sensitive hairs on their inner surfaces and are fringed with sharp bristles. If an insect touches one of these delicate hairs, the leaf snaps shut, holding the insect inside. Special glands then secrete special fluid which digests the insect. It's a deadly plant—described as carnivorous—and just one of the mysterious ways Mother Nature insures the preservation of life.

It's a gruesome image, but Venus's-flytrap illustrates the way psychological mechanisms can trap women into illusions of love. By the time we awaken, the damage is done. All over the world billions of women have been trapped in the natural cycle of preserving the race (the strongest genetic imperative). They are born, marry, and produce children until they die, not much above the level of animals. Their greatest struggle is for survival. They never have the opportunity to learn to read and write, much less to achieve personal consciousness and identity.

In the United States, particularly, teen-age girls are beguiled into patterns of romantic love—premature marriage, bearing several children, and then, in increasing numbers, early divorce. As a marriage and divorce counselor, I've been called in to try to preserve the pieces —either of the marriage or, if that's impossible, the persons involved. It's as though they've been trapped by some great and powerful force, sucked dry, and discarded. And often their first driving need is to repeat the process. Why? What traps women in emotional bondage in civilized countries long after they've escaped physiological bondage? The inescapable answer appears to be the power and the illusion of romantic love!

Like an arrow speeding toward its target or a jet plane streaking toward its destination, American women—and men—have been programmed for one form of love—romantic love. This illusion constitutes the deadliest barrier against women's growth and development. Love turns out to be women's sole purpose in life, with work done outside the home only in order to provide family necessities.

Yet we take for granted that men are free to develop in both areas. For them, work is on one side, and love is on the other. Women have been allowed to pursue only one side. It has been appropriate for spinsters to dedicate themselves to work, but marriage and work have not been considered compatible. For example, for years, school teachers were not allowed to marry. Married women have been forced by convention into making their love *both* their love and their work; yet

Freud once said that psychological health was marked by a person is being able *both* to love and to work. He kept wondering what women wanted and thought it was a penis. What I believe we want and need is a center in our being that allows us both to love and to work. By Freud's standards, women have been condemned to ill health because their pole of creative work has remained undeveloped.

The illusion of romantic love serves as the source of woman's continuing bondage and perpetuates her continuing immaturity. The deadliest emotional cycle circumscribes adolescents who "fall in love," marry, and awaken a few years, months, or weeks later to wonder what is wrong with them and their marriage since they are no longer "in love." They begin frantically searching for a replacement love in which they can "live happily ever after."

Inner mechanisms produce this psychological vulnerability, but I am more concerned right now about the sociological aspects. Our culture is geared to perpetuate this illusion. Turn on any all-day radio station that plays music, and you can chart the lines of popular songs which drum it into our unconscious memory-banks: "Can't take my eyes off of you," "can't live if living is without you," "more than you know," "my whole life depends on you," "I'm on the top of the world . . . only explanation is the love that I've found," "what are you doing the rest of your life . . . hope it all begins and ends with me."

Think of all the romantic heroes and heroines, of tragic, unrequited love, and of star-crossed lovers dying for each other: Romeo and Juliet, Jane Eyre and her melancholy master, Cathy and Heathcliff. Recall heroines like Scarlett O'Hara whose whole life, energy, and survival revolved first around Ashley and then around Rhett Butler.

Of all the various illusions in this country, romance is the most unquestioned. It is a billion-dollar business, leading to the largest diamond rings bridegrooms can afford, the most elaborate weddings the parents of brides can produce, and the most expensive, luxurious array of wedding gifts friends can bestow. We've gone from electric toasters to electric blankets to electric coffeepots and toothbrushes. Next what every young couple will need besides a crockpot will be an electric toenail clipper!

Young girls, despite the influences of the women's movement, still wait breathlessly until the right young man comes along to sweep them off their feet. Young men are engulfed in this national epidemic too. In *The Graduate,* Dustin Hoffman was catapulted into undying love even though he managed to resist the conveyor belt which would have led him straight from college into plastics.

We take for granted that the whole world loves young lovers. One might imagine archeologists from some other great intergalactic civilization someday patiently gluing back together those romantic silhouettes of couples walking along moonlit beaches and querying what strange sort of quadruped could have been photographed only in such settings. A different form of Loch Ness monster which only emerged at night?

But it is even more devastating that romantic love is such a matter of life and death. Romantic love consists of two alone against the world. The beloved becomes that one other person upon whom the lover places all needs and wants for personal fulfillment, warmth, and love. The first face of our mother, once the key to our survival as it bent over the bassinet, is replaced by the face of the loved one without whom life becomes meaningless. And, for those who have no belief in any God, such romances become idolatrous. One young man confessed to me frankly just after the death of his wife that he had been her god and she had been his. Few are that honest, but the accounts of those widowed or divorced, in books such as *Widow* and *One Man Hurt,* reveal that losing one's mate is losing the god upon whom everything in life depended. Today we do not allow widows to immolate themselves upon their husbands' burial pyres nor whole households to be buried with the great leaders who commanded them; yet statistics show an increased incidence of heart attacks and cancer among those recently bereaved. This suggests that, with the death of a loved one, often one's whole system gives up and dies anyway.

If our one, all-important, idolatrous love does not sustain us (which it never could), we move quickly to repeat the cycle, not to break it: love and marriage; unlove and divorce; love and marriage, and so on. Another billion-dollar industry thrives on the illusions of romantic love—the divorce-and-remarriage business. Formerly, people looked askance at so-called primitive chieftains who supported harems of several wives; today we are beginning to take for granted the pathetic men caught in the alimony bind of four or five ex-wives. When will he ever learn? people hoot. We accept too easily a frantic new form of musical-chair marriage; people keep trying on mates as if they were shoes in a store, dropping children right and left as they go. You may know marriages with mixed bags of children—his, hers, and theirs. Recently I heard of a "family" with seven children of which only two children had the same parents!

And the books proliferate. Somehow we suppose we can find just the right how-to manual that will give us instruction in remodeling ourselves into more attractive bait or tell us how to manipulate our mate into providing a more comfortable pumpkin shell. We grow restless in our illusions and rush around seeking the missing ingredient that will put us back onto the great American conveyor belt of romantic love.

In order to break the spell of romantic love and marriage, we have to look at it closely. How can what seems so normal and beautiful turn into genuine heartbreak and disillusionment? How can we recognize pitfalls of the romantic stage? What can we do when romance grows cold and our world shrinks and shrivels? If we suddenly discover we are suffocating in a confining marriage, does the marriage break or the person—like Mary Hartman?

The answers to these questions can be terribly painful. I know; I've worked through them all. When I married, I was high on love I knew would last forever. I could not imagine a time when those feelings would fade or change and I would have to leave them and move on. I presumed that romantic love would last forever. When it didn't, I had to search for explanations of the phenomenon which engulfed me.

The simplest explanation for romantic love would be that it is the springtime flowering of our need to find a mate. To stay within this period would prevent the maturation of the seed-buds of our deeper spirits.

But romantic love is more complex. It is a tangled skein of yearnings that we have to pick out, sort, and rearrange in order of priority. Some yearnings are genuine and legitimate: sex, companionship, intimacy, and sharing and working with a partner toward mutually-agreed-upon personal goals. But other yearnings are potentially disastrous: needing a private mutual admiration society; wanting a private household god—in the form of a mate; desiring a perennial parent, an all-encompassing container within whose love-shell our identities never have to mature; wishing for a partner to carry all our undeveloped parts, those we dare not nurture or that society will not allow (for example, women used to go to seminary and then marry a minister instead of becoming one); and needing to project ourselves onto someone who meets enough of our idealized needs to reflect the person we desire to see in ourselves. This last yearning is a narcissistic need that can lead to demonic forms of possessiveness.

Behind these elements is the common motif of an incompleted identity crisis. During adolescence we should mature into ourselves and not feel split between good and bad or male and female, that is, beyond normal sexual attributes. Romantic love is partly the attraction between two half-developed persons who meet and supposedly make one whole. The boy (not yet a man) gets to carry and live out all the attributes allowed males in his culture—strength, assertiveness, power, and control. The girl (not yet a woman) gets to carry all the attributes allowed females—tenderness, passivity, and childishness. He may become the strong hero father and she the sweet daughter; or she may become the great mother and he her miraculous son.

As long as each does not grow, the spell may last indefinitely; but if one partner begins to mature, the spell is broken. The other must then search for a replacement to match up things the way they used to be. The imperative need is to fill the gap.

Behind the spell of romantic love is often a dependent person who has not yet been able to develop to full human capacity. The barrier society has placed against women's growth and development condemns both men and women to repeat romantic spells.

One beautiful illustration of how a woman can be caught in such a spell was the television series "I Dream of Jeannie." This amusing little bit of fluff, a situation comedy, began appearing nationally in prime time back in 1965. A fascinating genie was found and released from two thousand years of captivity when an American astronaut landed near a deserted tropical island after a space mission. The astronaut, Captain Anthony Nelson, picked up her bottle, opened it, and attempted to leave her on the island, but Jeannie followed him back to Cocoa Beach, Florida, where she continued to play "Spin the Astronaut."

Nelson wanted to set her free, but Jeannie insisted that she now belonged to him. He couldn't get rid of her. In order to get her way —which was to capture him for her own—she was willing to placate his needs any way she could.

One early problem Jeannie faced was luring the captain away from his fiancée, Melissa. Melissa personified the woman who seeks to dominate a man directly, who insists upon having her way and is incapable of understanding a man's needs. Although equally intent upon getting her way, Jeannie was more subtle. She constantly attended her man. She anticipated his needs and insinuated her way into his life in such a way that he was totally impotent to assert himself. Her methods were indirect, oblique, manipulative—and inevitably effective. He wound up being totally responsible for her, having to drop his work to care for her needs whenever she began loosing pieces of herself. In one episode he had to appear in Mecca with her to renew her powers of geniehood.

In an early segment Nelson was being debriefed by the staff psychiatrist immediately following the mission in which he'd found Jeannie. He admitted having had a strange experience as if it had been an hallucination. He explained how the genie he found had not been just "run of the mill" but beautiful, desirable, helpful, and attentive to his every need. Dr. Bellows diagnosed Nelson's story in Freudian terms: a classic Oedipal fantasy every male child has about his mother.

The Jungian branch of psychology, however, would say that Jeannie represented more than a mother figure for Tony. She would be termed the living embodiment of his undeveloped feminine side. In the growth and development of consciousness, there is a period when this feminine side of men is completely unconscious and projected upon the mother. The more unconscious it is, however, the more powerful is its attraction for the male.

Unfortunately, a woman caught playing the role necessarily suffers from the same level of undeveloped consciousness. Her undeveloped masculine side is in turn projected upon him. This combination of projections creates one of the most powerful aspects of romantic love.

In later years, however, the woman who has not found herself, is naturally and unconsciously trapped into playing the role of the pure feminine for the man. Neither man nor woman has reached any real consciousness of themselves. Both can be drawn into a relationship which preserves the pattern—in fact, it takes two to perpetuate it. Both are trapped in a repetitive pattern they cannot escape. Both are "unliberated."

Several books have been published recently which are devoted entirely to teaching women how to play this feminine role for men more effectively and consciously. The first, *Fascinating Womanhood,* was written by Helen B. Andelin and published about the time "I Dream of Jeannie" appeared on television; the second, *The Total Woman* by Marabel Morgan, came out eight years later. By mid-1975, sales of both books had reached over two million copies, and thousands of women were signing up for courses in how to preserve a perfect marriage based upon romantic illusions. It was even rumored that large corporations and the U.S. State Department were contracting for such courses to train wives of their executives. Imagine what it might do to a man's ego if, in the middle of an important business deal, his wife were to call and murmur huskily in his ear, "I crave your body!"

It's a beautiful illusion. Take one wife, dress her in cowboy boots, ruffled, black-sequin apron, and sexy perfume—period. Have her greet her man each night at the door with a perfectly chilled martini and provocatively shadowed eyelids—just like Jeannie. Teach her all the harem tricks—to think only of her man and his needs. Never allow her to murmur one unkind word or think one unkind thought. Perhaps it's worth it to have the Miami Dolphins win more football games or to have more astronauts soaring happily in space. But will the divorce rate drop? I doubt it. And I would predict an increased number of women alcoholics and cases of depression and suicide.

Books such as *The Total Woman* do legitimate sex and take it out of the closet for many women who never considered themselves sexual creatures, but basically they perpetuate the most deadly illusion in the Western world. They send wives back to repeat the adolescent spell of romantic love. Too often they begin thinking, "What is wrong with me? Why can't I be happy with a bigger refrigerator and having sex every night at eleven? What's awry in my pumpkin shell? What should Peter do to help me feel better?"

The need women have to repeat courses in fascinating or total womanhood reflects the unreality of perpetuating one stage in life long after it could have been outgrown and the difficulty of remaining in such a developmental stage. Ironically, the task of assuming responsibility for consciously playing the role can lead to increased consciousness and heightened awareness of conscious choices—which can in turn lead to satiation, boredom, and frustration.

SPELLS AROUND MOTHERHOOD

Normal Need: To fulfill one's emotional and physiological potential for motherhood.
Normal Pattern of Growth: The procreation and nurture of children during the years when they need protection and support, followed by a period of emotional weaning for the child and mother.
Distortion or Spell: Continuance of normal mothering beyond the time of fulfilling needs of very young children; failing to wean either one's children or one's self.

In my collection of pictures of women, two particularly poignant ones perfectly represent the double bind in which women find themselves. In the first a young mother nurses her child while her husband sits close beside her. This tender portrait evokes unconscious parallels to paintings of Madonna and child in previous centuries. The love between the parents is obviously real and meaningful, as is their mutual concern for the child. This picture represents all that can be positive and good about the mothering period in a woman's life.

The second picture disturbs everyone who sees it. It symbolizes all that is problematical about mothering. The wife/mother is in the background, smiling with a fawning, sick expression on her face. Her attention is devoted to the two children and their father. They sit some distance from her, concentrating on a globe of the world. She is literally "out of it," passively waiting for them to need her. She is not reading or even doing some homely task such as mending socks or putting up a hem but is focusing entirely on the three loved ones who are oblivious to her.

This woman has been caught in the spell of Earth Mother. Her children are past the age of needing her constant attention. She has obviously done a good job of caring for them and for her husband. They appear healthy and well clothed. An immaculate house fills the background. She has fulfilled all the imperatives our culture has placed upon women through magazines and television commercials.

She is now at the edge of possible new growth and development. What fantasies might you have for her? What will she do with her new-found time? Obvious affluence suggests she needn't work for money alone. She has the potential to do anything she wishes: volunteer work, creative arts, further study toward a new vocation or new skills.

Unfortunately she may do nothing. I have known many women like this. They have had all the children they plan to have. They look at the job markets closing in and question the value of further study or training for jobs. They question the advisability of entering the mainstream at this point in their lives. Here and there they dabble a bit in volunteer work or fill their days with leisure activities such as golf, bridge, shopping, or sewing. These women maintain the ongoing threads in the loom of society, while the men and children in their lives weave the pattern. They remain in the wings, while others take center stage. They are good people, good women, good wives, and good mothers—but trapped in the unconscious spell of Earth Mother.

In primitive cultures, Earth Mothers die young, exhausted by years of childbearing and poor nutrition. In our culture, Earth Mothers live on, often failing to wean their children, but even more often having to draw into their webs new children in the form of worthy projects and committee meetings. The former usually creates a lot of busy work, and the latter generally accomplishes little and even fails to provide real interpersonal contact. For years I lived half-in and half-out of this world; I know its seductive power firsthand. The simplest, happiest time of my life was probably the nine years during which my four children were born. I remember the thrill of each birth and the heartwarming days when I was too busy to think beyond the household routines of cooking, cleaning, sewing, shopping, and playing with children. But those days came to a close with the Caesarian birth of my fourth child, and I realized I could not forever fill my life with bearing and caring for children.

Earth Mothers come in all sizes, shapes, colors, and ages, although they differ in terms of how much and how long motherhood overwhelms them. But two traits characterize them all: a lack of individual identity and overidentification with children and family. These two factors are co-related: without personal identity, one turns to others for a vicarious identity; the more successfully one lives out the role of Earth Mother, the less she feels a need to develop her inner being. The outer "mother" role substitutes for an inner sense of self. All inner energy and outer activities and drive are concentrated upon motherhood. She has no time for anything or anybody else outside the immediate family. She is often content to remain year in and year out within the close confines of her home. This attitude affects not only what she consciously does and thinks, but also what she unconsciously expects in return from other people.

What is apt to impress us most about a woman caught in the spell of Earth Mother is that she appears to be unconscious of herself. She is absorbed by important others in her life. She is constantly doing things for them, giving out of an overflowing abundance. She considers this her sole purpose in life. She is the giver, never the receiver.

There are several hitches to this form of generosity. First, such giving to others does not come from a sense of her individuality but from her overidentification with others. Because she is unconsciously one with the other, she is really giving just as much to herself as to the other.

You may righteously protest, "But giving and doing for others is a good thing." True, real giving and doing is good, but it must be free and easy with no unconscious expectations of return. An Earth Mother's giving and doing carries an expensive price tag. Her gifts and deeds are done with the expectation that they are just what the recipient wants—and with the added kicker that he/she will do and be just what Earth Mother expects. She builds a fine network of dependent lines between herself and others and then begins pulling on those lines to get them to do and be exactly as she expects, with a subtle look, or a raised eyebrow, or a blatant "After all I've done for you, . . ."

Her overidentification with the other person means she cannot tolerate behavior different from her own. She imposes a heavy load of shame and guilt if the other fails to do as she says. She assumes that she knows what they are thinking and that they ought to know what she is thinking.

The double bind is that the other persons involved are just as unconscious as she is of the potentially real person she might be. And they often continue to ignore her being a separate person long after she has begun to awaken from the spell. She is an invisible woman for them. One friend said wistfully, "I'm so tired of being the hub of the wheel in the family; I would like to be just one of the spokes." It's devastating when couples take each other for granted; it's deadly when children take a mother for granted long after she has consciously attempted to wean them.

For example, Nina Lake was the mother of six children. Her youngest child had just entered high school, and Nina could see a new life ahead. Then the two oldest children came back home to live. Twenty-five-year-old Maria had left her husband, and Jimmy, twenty-three, had lost his job and run out of money. Nina felt depressed, angry, hopeless. When would she ever have time for herself?

In soap-opera land we find the best Earth Mother specimens in captivity. For years no self-respecting soap could keep going without one key figure, the mother-wife around whom a whole world of problems revolved as she concentrated on the endless details of personal existence: who was in love with whom, who was marrying whom, who was having a child, whose heart was breaking because of a faithless lover or an ungrateful son or daughter. Examples of the good, sweet, pure woman permeated the soaps, as did Bad Mothers, those who failed to fulfill the traditional image.

But even the soaps are changing. Since 1965 Edith Horton ("Days of Our Lives") has reigned as Earth Mother supreme, but in 1975 she began to emerge as a human being with a few character flaws. Her unfounded suspicion of granddaughter Julie's behavior led to Edith's subsequent loss of faith in God and in herself. It was good to see her dealing with the real world.

What the soaps have never shown is that the power of good Earth Mother is even more insidious than Bad Mother's. It is easy to walk out on a patently selfish, manipulative woman who schemes, bribes, cajoles, and cons her victims. It's infinitely harder to see the seductiveness of Earth Mother and how she perpetuates her children's dependence. Such women are the archetypal source of stories about heroes slaying the awful dragon in order to rescue maiden-victim. The only way Perseus could slay Medusa was with a mirror; otherwise he would have fallen under her spell. In Jungian psychology, the power of the dragon often represents man's deep incestuous longing to maintain a symbiotic relationship with the mother. During the first Axial Age (800–400 B.C.) rational ego consciousness was freed from the former participation mystique which was common for early, tribal, nonhistorical man who had been trapped in the cyclical patterns of nature and Mother Earth. Patriarchy, a debatable alternative, was established over against matriarchal origins. Today we are on the brink of a second Axial Age as women become a new breed of mothers, first conscious of themselves as persons and thus able to mother appropriately.

CHAPTER 3

Spell Breaking

THE INVISIBLE WOMAN

A woman caught in a spell so that her real identity cannot develop is an invisible woman. She is playing out a role of which she is completely unconscious. If she is under Earth Mother's spell, she has been trapped by the needs of the race for survival; she is powerless to free herself from the pattern these needs impose. Everything does seem to happen to her. Her ego (rational self) never developed because emotional binds restricted it. It is not surprising that primitive socieites emphasize fate, for the group is trapped in a level of collective unconsciousness. Women trapped in this stage of life likewise are fascinated by TV game shows in which so much depends upon Lady Luck and so little upon real competence and skill.

Whatever spell they may be caught in, their invisibility makes many of these women seem alike. Their outer shell presents a façade of stereotyped superficiality—clothes, hair styles, make-up. Fashion is important because the outer shell must meet the external whims of social expectations. Keeping up with the Joneses is important because these women project all standards and authority to those outside themselves.

But on the inside, these women remain undeveloped. External pressures confine them and keep them spellbound. Lacking a sense of selfhood and an opportunity to develop individual talents and abilities, they share a common state of immaturity, childishness, and pettiness. Little trifles become overwhelmingly important because nothing more demanding has been expected of them. They spend an agonizing amount of time worrying over what color to paint the living room, what to serve guests for dinner, what to do and where to go for entertainment. They may call their husbands at work two, three, four, or more times daily. They may spend many empty hours with friends, playing bridge, tennis, golf, or shopping, if they can afford it. If they can't and must work, most perform stale repetitive tasks in factories, stores, and offices with little hope for advancement or change.

These women are caught in emotional arith-ME-tic, struggling over how to add and subtract when it comes to emotional problems. They come for counseling, expecting to be told explicitly what to do with their lives and then stare blankly if asked a question beyond their experience. They appear to have no conception that they could do something concretely themselves, that they could prevent what always seems to be *happening to* them. Somewhere, somebody must exist who can fix things up, pour something into their lives to make up for the void caused by an undeveloped self. Their inner poverty constitutes the single most-undeveloped resource in the world.

THE LEADING EDGE

The leading edge of the women's movement is not with the one and one-half million women who have bought Betty Friedan's *The Feminine Mystique* or with those who subscribe to *Ms.* or belong to NOW. These women are working actively out of a personal conviction of their selfhood which will not accept a socioeconomic, political system which denies them full rights and responsibilities in achieving the American dream as they visualize it.

The women who are just beginning to grow and who fear moving out of present patterns are at the real growing edge, such as the two and one-half million women studying how to be totally fascinating; and the women caught in the spells described earlier. They need to awaken, to glimpse a new image of themselves as persons, and to envision a wider horizon in their lives.

When a spell starts to break up, a woman begins to have feelings she has not anticipated. On the surface, her life may have been going along smoothly, but suddenly everything's a bit out of kilter. Feeling a little strange, she wonders, "What's the matter with me?" She may feel bored, restless, frustrated, or depressed when there's no apparent reason. Or she may feel empty and blank and begin to search for something to fill the gap. She may begin to blame people around her for what's going on inside herself. "If only Harry would change and be the way he used to be!" "If only my children would behave better to me!" "If only someone would give me a rewarding, satisfying job!"

Sometimes spells break up because of personal disaster. The death of a husband or child brings more than bereavement and requires more than a period of mourning. The "better" half is missing, the half that supplied life-focus and protected the undeveloped self. Divorce can create the same effect. A husband, exhausted by his wife's clinging, finally shakes loose, almost as if it were his survival or hers.

Regardless of how or why a spell begins to break up, there are emotional side-effects. These are symptoms of potential growth. This opportunity may be met straight on and recognized, or it may be denied in the hope it will go away, but inner growth cannot really be denied. It is "fascinating" to me that both Marabel Morgan and Helen Andelin admitted feelings of dissatisfaction with their own marriages. Then they set about to invent programs to recapture romantic love, systems for inspiring "celestial love" (Andelin) and for inside "interior decorating" (Morgan). Paradoxically, next both women set about to teach their systems as experts, to become nationally famous authors. This meant that neither remained within the traditional pattern of the simple little housewife, entirely devoted to husband and pumpkin shell.

As old systems and spells break down, women turn for help outside home or work. They seek the advice of experts. On one level they turn to interior decorators, hairdressers, new clothes, courses in new skills (crewel, bargello, tennis, golf, pottery, painting), or travel. On a deeper level they turn to physical and mental health professionals: to medical doctors for relief from migraines, menopausal disorders, colitis, or skin allergies; to counselors for relief from emotional discomfort and lack of inner ease. Still others, more despairing, turn silently within, relying on chemotherapy—alcohol and/or uppers and downers to provide highs their life-styles have denied them.

ATTENTION MUST BE PAID

Toward the end of Arthur Miller's play *The Death of a Salesman,* Mrs. Willie Loman says about her husband: "Attention must be paid." Similarly, attention must be paid to Matildas and the other women caught in spells. In fact, they insist on attention in a variety of ways, the first indication of the potential breakdown of old spells.

They first claim attention because of painful symptoms, sometimes physical, but more often emotional—boredom, depression, restlessness, frustration, emptiness, and suffocation. These signs indicate a movement within the psyche toward growth and wholeness. The old patterns are too limited, too confining, too cramped.

Often, of course, a woman insists that the problem is outside herself. Something is *happening to* her. Some relationship has gone sour; something is wrong with *somebody* else. Or something is wrong with her body; in a detached way, she says the "head" aches or the "system" doesn't function. To suggest directly that this is untrue would be a mistake. Her pain is real and needs attention. On the surface her problem is "outside," but its source lies within—her inner spirit needs to grow.

If symptoms are taken for the limit of her problem, a woman is apt to be locked into variations on the old spells and to fall into a new spell with a slightly different cast of characters.

GENERAL SPELLS OUTSIDE FAMILY LIFE

Normal Need: Meaningful activities and relationships.
Normal Pattern of Growth: Away from the dependency of childhood into the dependability of adult.
Distortion or Spell: Dependency during the entire life cycle.

Women who never marry and have children, as well as women who have lost loved ones upon whom they were dependent, may still remain in a permanent Me state of mind. Although they may live independently and may appear to function normally, they actually may be caught in one of two permanent spells: Patient or Red Cross Nurse. In both, the woman has not developed as a person and assumes a permanent life-script in which she plays one continuing role very well.

In the Patient role, the spell consists of two figures: woman herself and Rescuer, the new authority figure to whom she begins running to be saved. When one problem or symptom is solved, she invents another. She plays the role of *patient* sufferer seeking relief. If she goes for counseling, the therapist may see through her attempts to find a Wizard or Good Witch to solve her problems, but other helpers or friends are not likely to understand the game she plays. The therapist's task focuses on helping Patient learn to develop the inner capacity to stand on her own two feet, discover alternative life-styles, and begin to outgrow passive dependency.

For example, Mona Brown (described in chap. 1) would stare incredulously at me if I asked, "Did you ever think you might be able to go shopping by yourself?" Her interpretation was that her husband didn't "care" for her if he didn't care to take her shopping. She couldn't understand that he could care for her in other ways, although he had outgrown wanting to care for her as a dependent child. He needed her to be a whole person; she blamed him for not treating her as a child. She felt put upon all the time. No one was "caring" for her, and she couldn't grasp the idea that it was time for her to care for herself.

It's hard to imagine that a grown woman of forty-two couldn't get up and get dressed in the morning so she could ride to work with her husband, shop, and then take a bus back home by herself—or that she didn't want to learn to drive. She had been programmed to stay at home, completely dependent and therefore frustrated beyond belief. No wonder she was angry and nobody could please her. She had never learned to please herself.

Session after session she complained about how badly everyone treated her; session after session I acknowledged her frustration and hurt but then began to question her so that she might start accounting for her self and her choices. She needed to examine how she was contributing to her unhappiness. When had she been happy? Had she ever worked? Yes, as an office clerk. How did she feel about herself when she was working? She had liked having her own money and the freedom that allowed. How did she account for needing her husband so much now? Could she see any way she might begin doing something for herself?

Mona was hurting; yet she could not get in touch with how she played into the situation that hurt her. She needed to gain space of her own, ground to stand on, and goals for the future. However, these things had to grow out of her self. Anything I supplied, beyond attention and concern, would deprive her again—just as parents and teachers had done in allowing her to be a dependent child instead of an autonomous, responsible being.

The flip side of Patient Spell/Game/Script is Permanent Parent-/Nurse/Wizard/Witch. We all know such energetic women—Super-Moms, female rescuers, Red Cross Nurse. Their grand desire is to see all, hear all, rescue all. They have the answers and the control. Ken Kesey created Big Nurse to perfection in *One Flew over the Cuckoo's Nest.* In the movie, actress Louise Fletcher captured the indomitable spirit of Big Nurse with her complete incapacity to see another as a person other than a child/patient whom she must protect at all costs from them-*selves.*

Red Cross Nurse is the feminine version of Wizard with one exception—the patient martyrdom which such women exhibit. They are pure Madonnas, dispensing sweetness and light; everyone else takes advantage of them. They give, give, give. They don't allow themselves to become angry at the injustice others have done to them, at the way they get taken advantage of, at the endless draining of their resources with no sense of reciprocal give-and-take. Inside them lingers an ungrown child who longs to take, take, take and who never can be filled.

Not many women caught in the spell of Red Cross Nurse ever seek counseling. They are too busy being Rescuers themselves. If their physical health breaks down, they turn to physical remedies for their dis-eases and symptoms. Otherwise they perform like a gyroscope that got turned on one day and keeps endlessly spinning, spinning, spinning.

Maxine Black, the gifted pianist described in chapter 1, had given up a potential career in order to stay at home and preserve her marriage. She thought her husband's ego couldn't take her increasing professional success, and so she dropped out of a concert circuit and raised three sons.

Maxine was in "battle" with her husband over who would play Red Cross Nurse and who would play Patient. Her problem began when she began turning to alcohol as the years went by in order to "preserve" herself and her husband. She was frustrated, not knowing how to recapture a sense of herself as a talented musician. She was certain she couldn't rebuild her career; she had no imagination for dreaming up other musical outlets.

So she was staying at home even though her children were grown. Her inner frustration was eating her alive and driving her and her husband to drink. She believed the problem was her husband's fault. He kept taking from her, deceiving her, playing around. He didn't deserve all she had given up for him. She would stay to preserve him, of course, as Red Cross Nurse, because she couldn't conceive any other role for herself. If she could save him, then she would be saving herself—from facing herself.

Maxine is caught in one spell along the yellow brick road. Like Dorothy, she expects her husband (the Wizard) to be all and do all, to fill her needs indirectly. He refuses to let her be Patient, however, and has begun drinking heavily himself.

Maxine can't see her alcoholic pattern as an evasion of emotional responsibility. Her feelings of inadequacy are too great to permit her to dig up skills, talents, and interests and begin fulfilling her own needs directly. Tragically she is becoming an alcoholic, in desperate competition with her husband. Instead of beginning to "compete" positively for professional recognition, she is fighting him over the role of alcoholic. Until she can face her inner wicked witch of the West and destroy her self-destructive impulses, the musical world will continue to be deprived of her talents, and she will remain spellbound.

TWO CHOICES

Two doors—repetition and growth—wait in front of Mona, Maxine, and all the other Matildas. The first opens into other spells and continuing enchantment. The second opens into the risky realm of self-examination, learning to stand on one's own two feet, and space to grow in. This doesn't mean giving up important personal relationships. It does not mean isolation, but a shift to richer, deeper intimacy based on mutuality and sharing instead of dependency and role playing.

The choice is between breaking old spells and moving on or staying locked in for life. Sociologist Kurt Lewin and anthropologist Margaret Mead have pointed out that the question can never be, How can we change people? but rather, How do people change? Change and growth come slowly and painfully and require work.

STAGE II

Time for Myself

The most important period in our development as persons is the Myself stage. In this time of transition we shift out of the Me state of mind and begin to find our selves as persons. Ideally this stage occurs during adolescence. As young persons separate from their families and identify with peer groups and role leaders, testing and trying out their identities, they are asking, Who am I? But girls often stay in the Me state of mind, moving unconsciously from being at home with their parents to being at home with their husbands, staying within a protective shell which keeps them from finding themselves.

Going through the Myself stage in adulthood means dealing with many new feelings. Often we are caught between the depression and boredom we want to be rid of and guilt and shame if we assert ourselves. Learning to deal with these feelings is a major task if we want to cease being dependent on others for identity and to create our own center of being.

49

CHAPTER 4

To Be or Not to Be?

THE IN-BETWEEN TIME

Moving outward from the Me stage can be the most exciting time in a woman's life as far as her personal growth and development are concerned. This period, the Myself stage, is full of emotional ups and downs, highs and lows, good and bad feelings. This is a time of *self-discovery* as we work through new tasks and begin exercising new muscles of selfhood, a time of *becoming* when we reach out to own parts of our selves which have been lost or stolen, a time of *centering* within instead of being satellites of somebody else.

The most significant feature of the Myself stage is its in-between quality. Quite literally, it is between Me and I stages. Through it, we move away from the passivity and dependency of the Me stage and toward the I stage characterized by fullness of selfhood. But the Myself stage is an uneven growth period. Just as we think we are making progress, we discover we have taken a giant emotional step backward. Nevertheless, the Myself stage is essential to personal maturation, and unfortunately it has been denied many women. One would hope that it will be taken for granted as part of each person's heritage as our understanding of human development continues to advance.

However, many women bypassed this period in their formative years, and now, as wives, mothers, and/or working women, they must

51

rework the basic tasks of selfhood. Erik H. Erikson has described the major developmental tasks each person faces during the human life-cycle. If we use his classifications as a guide, it is clear that many women have failed to move normally through the basic growth crises. Through no initial fault of their own, they remained in the school of *I*dentity, repeating kindergarten level tasks.

During the Myself stage women must perform developmental tasks which under normal circumstances they would have completed in earlier years. For example, gaining enough self-confidence and autonomy to be able to exercise initiative without having an all-pervading sense of shame or guilt is the basic task of early childhood. During elementary school children gradually form a sense of self-worth based upon genuine competence and industry. A woman who failed to accomplish this must deal with a continuing sense of inferiority, inadequacy, and frustration. In adolescence the major developmental task is establishing a sense of self. Women have been held back particularly in this task and have had to settle for a secondhand, indirect, or derived identity based upon being somebody's daughter, wife, or mother. During adolescence genuine feelings of personal uniqueness based upon real skills of ego-mastery need to be established; many women skip this phase altogether in the process of falling in love, marrying, and having children. Later they have to pick up their postponed developmental tasks, as if they'd been on a long detour through the fields of wife and motherhood.

FEELINGS

In working through these tasks, feelings surface which may be very difficult to handle: *anxiety and fear* as we move away from dependence on another, *self-doubt and shame* because we are inexperienced and unprepared for a new way of life; *guilt* that we may be disappointing others' expectations and breaking unwritten laws of our social group.

We have to deal directly with these feelings. Some stem from our innate sense of timing in growth and development. They must be listened to sincerely so that we move ahead slowly and steadily without overextending ourselves too soon. We have to learn to trust these feelings and ourselves.

But other strong feelings actually come from the internalized voices of important people in our past—voices of parents, relatives, teachers, old friends who imposed on us their standards of merit and worth without giving us a chance to develop our own. We often feel self-doubt, shame, and guilt because we still fear disappointing these people. Such feelings can serve as fences which corral us within boundary lines others have laid out. Every time we bump up against such a feeling, we need to ask, Is that my own stuff or is it a guilt feeling somebody laid on me a long time ago? We need to trust that we can be warm, loving persons who can care both for ourselves and for others simultaneously and not worry that caring for ourselves needs to conflict with caring for others.

THE PROBLEM OF SELF-ISHNESS

One of the most difficult problems women face, especially if they have been extremely dependent upon another person, is the problem of *self-ishness.* They generally feel they cannot manage to be good to themselves and grow without depriving others. Their natural instinct is based on the shortage-economy principle: There is only a certain amount of caring to go around. Because of this, they continue to focus on others and ignore themselves.

For example, when did you last buy yourself a little treat? It might have been just a small thing—a real rose or carnation to put on the table where you eat, a magazine containing a really inviting article, a real hot lunch downtown instead of the usual "brown bag." Or it might have been something bigger, something that really stretched your budget. I can remember the first hardback book I bought myself during the days when we had three children and couldn't even afford to go out to a movie. I felt particularly guilty and "selfish" because the book was *Atlas Shrugged,* an immensely long novel about a woman who fought to do her own thing well and to be her own person. And I always felt guilty when I went out in the daytime without one of the children. I could take one child alone to the dentist and leave the others home alone or with a sitter, but I could never take time off alone without having real guilt feelings or fearing something horrendous might happen to one of them while I was gone.

It was especially hard when I started back in graduate school. I was only taking two courses at a time. At most I was away from the children about eight hours a week, but I had to struggle to balance homework and homelife. It was hard enough without all those guilt feelings about being selfish. Then Betty Friedan's *The Feminine Mystique* came out. I recognized myself in those pages and began to feel I wasn't really so strange after all in wanting to develop my mind instead of becoming more and more proficient at cooking and sewing. For years I made all the dresses for my first two daughters and myself. I had become a pretty good seamstress and cook (although I was— and continue to be—a poor housekeeper), but that wasn't quite enough for the rest of my life. Friedan's book opened a door I needed right then as support in the new life I had already started.

But the next thing I knew, I received a letter from Peggy, my former mother-in-law. She enclosed an article about Friedan and her book. Written along the top above the headline was "What a selfish woman!" I was devastated. My newfound sense of self was ripped apart. I had admired and honored Peggy for years, endeavoring to be like her in many ways. My mother had worked until I was ten, and I had missed the sort of mother-at-home Peggy had been. She was college educated, a former teacher, active in community and church work, a truly wonderful person. She had been my role-model, a woman who had raised two sons and then gone on to other creative work. How could she say that Betty Friedan was selfish? Of course, I extrapolated and thought she also meant I was selfish in going back to school.

Fortunately I was able to work through this problem with the therapist I had begun seeing about my conflict about going back to school. With his support I realized that Peggy's comment bothered me because I actually had the same questions inside myself. Friedan's book had reinforced my needs and wants to continue to grow. In retrospect I understand that my being so influenced at that time by outside authorities was an indication of how dependent I still really was.

The counseling I received helped me break through the basic misunderstanding most people have about selfishness. Somehow I had unconsciously been going along with the shortage-economy principle, behaving as if caring for people was an either-or proposition. If I cared for another person would mean I was unselfish and was not caring for myself; if I cared for myself, I was selfish and uncaring for others. Actually, the more I am able to reach down into my own self and perceive my real feelings, needs, and wants and begin to satisfy them, the more I can do the same for others and begin to hear them. By enriching my life, I have more to share with others.

The concept of *selfishness* needs to be separated from *self-aggrandisement* and the search for personal control and power over others which is *selfish. To be good to one's self is not selfish.* To love only oneself is *narcissism;* to behave as if one were the only person in the world is *infantile omnipotence.* To be a whole person and to bloom and flower as a whole self is being human. The more we realize ourselves, the more we will work to help and encourage others to do so. Depriving myself will not help another grow or make up what he or she is missing, for we each have one life to grow in, one unique pattern in which to be our self.

GUILT AND SHAME

However, something else was going on inside me, something greater than the problem of *selfishness,* which helps explain the power such accusations have over us. Deep within me was a tug of war between two styles of life, two modes of child rearing, two forms of guilt and shame. I was caught in an impasse between them.

In order to break free, I had to really listen to each side. On the one hand, I was deeply attracted to Peggy's way of life. I had always yearned to have a mommy like the mommies of my little girlfriends, a mommy who stayed at home all day and was always there whether I needed her or not, a mommy who was really an all-giving Earth Mother. Yet, on the other hand my mother's having to work had allowed me the freedom to learn how to take care of myself in a way most little girls are not allowed. For years, I failed to recognize that as a rare gift. I never quite understood other little girls who sat back and did nothing, who had no initiative or creativity to get out and do something new when it was needed. Yet I was on the "outside," not they, and those childhood feelings of separateness had left me vulnerable to that pattern of life. I was caught by the typical social group standards that said I should have had the sort of emotional footbinding they had. My early freedom led to my later insecurity about being different.

Most little children, however, have not had that freedom to develop and test behavior. Like gardeners with huge pruning shears, parents and teachers stand ready to nip off any behavior or idea that offends them and threatens the only pattern of life they know. How many times have you heard:

"We don't do things like that in our house!"

"Why you wouldn't want to do a thing like that."

"What could you be thinking of?"

"You ought to be ashamed of yourself."

"Don't make me mad!"

Snip, snip, snip. Those kinds of commands and questions force a child to conform, just like a yew bush can be cut into the shape of a vase or a bunny rabbit and not be allowed to grow into its own unique shape. Since children are absolutely dependent upon parents, they learn to be passive and obedient and to disown anything which causes them distress. They learn to be ashamed and guilty of their own being. They learn the parents' way of life because they fear the loss of parental support and love.

The net effect is to stunt the growth of the child's eyes, ears, and sensitivity to perceive and analyze and to bind his or her spirit. The child will fail to develop essential ego skills for survival as an autonomous adult. The child will sacrifice the self out of love and fear of the loss of love. A girl will grow up to be a half-person, a Matilda. Such passivity in a child results in an apathetic woman who, out of a learned sense of powerlessness, cannot care for or be responsible for herself.

Today effectiveness training is enabling parents and teachers to avoid crippling children in the future. As these important people develop such skills as making *I* statements for the sake of their children, they are developing their own latent capacities which were deprived and crippled when they were children. They are also modeling new positive ways of behaving and speaking for children to imitate.

We have to move out of the fear of false shame and guilt. We need to view human growth as part of each person's inherent responsibility and to face a different kind of shame and guilt from another direction —from our failure not to grow, not to become, not to be whole creative persons who can be responsible in love for both ourselves and others.

Authority figures in our lives may have feared that we would upset their little worlds, precarious empires built out of the scripts and roles they were playing and the spells in which they were caught. I believe the fascination we all have with such phenomena as amnesia, impersonation, and acting results from our unconscious insight that there is a real difference between outer roles and inner reality. In this inner reality we are all equal. Mark Twain demonstrated the equality of the prince and the pauper behind the clothes they wore.

There is an authentic shame and guilt. It comes from a sense of *I*dentity because it can only be carried by the *I* which has developed to that degree. Real guilt and shame measures the failure to achieve potential more than the pettiness of previous deeds. It parallels the sharing that is only possible when one has a deep sense of self and possessions. You may have seen how cheerfully and graciously a small girl of two will give and give. Months later she develops a sense of ownership and self (hopefully). Until her ego grows a bit and she learns about the even greater possibilities of sharing reciprocally and working together, it will be very difficult for her to share. So also with our sense of ourselves. First we grow and develop a self, which means that for a while we have to discount all the old *shoulds* and *oughts* which compelled our former behavior. We have to disregard the old *musts* while we learn to listen for the still small voice of our true conscience which can only come from our deepest self. Then earlier forms of shame and guilt will be cast off, and we can rely on a sense of true justice and fairness for both ourselves and others.

FEARS

In the movie of *The Wizard of Oz,* as Dorothy and her friends follow the yellow brick road into the deep, dark forest, they sing, "Lions and tigers and bears, lions and tigers and bears . . ." Likewise, as we venture along inner paths of growth in the Myself stage, we are often beset with "lions and tigers and bears"—fears, anxieties, and even a potential sense of dread. We do not know what lies before us. We have lived comfortably in the Me cocoon where everything that happened to us could be blamed on someone else.

Now we have to move under our own control and direction. The unknown is frightening and scary. While the known may have been suffocating, it *was known* and reliable as long as we managed not to rock the boat.

What are our lions and tigers and bears? We can list them quickly, but learning to deal with them takes a while longer. We fear the lion of loss of support; we fear the tiger of the lack of control, of being overwhelmed, and of being confused without any sense of direction; we fear the bear of separation anxiety and being alone in a strange dark world.

I have heard enough women in growth groups speak about such fears to know that they are genuine. Facing personal unknowns is like standing on the edge of a forest or a cliff or a desert without any trails.

Women have been handicapped as persons. They have an "inner barrenness" instead of the rich variety of ego skills needed to survive, as Edrita Fried points out in *Active/Passive*. Like the little crippled boy in Laura Burnett's *Secret Garden,* they have lived in one "psychological" room. Their dependency on others feels just as real as a child's. They have been cramped and confined within their pumpkin shells, spells, womb-worlds, and Me security. Dealing with such fears requires facing and acknowledging them realistically and then proceeding one step at a time into the unknown.

One reason these fears can overwhelm is that we merge a lot of different worries and think we cannot tackle them all at once. We need to sort out specific fears and deal with them one at a time. Phyllis Carey, a young divorcée, was overwhelmed by a multitude of concerns. She was raising a young son and worried that she wouldn't be a good mother. She hated the job she had and worried that she would never be able to find a better one. Her apartment was on a busy street, and there were few children for her son to play with; she worried she'd never find another place to live. Her mother was ill, and she worried that she wasn't being a good daughter. She was pulled apart by all these worries—and immobilized—not daring to do anything about any one of them because she lumped them all together.

Gradually Phyllis realized that if she worked through them one at a time she could begin to overcome them. She first sorted out her alternatives in each dilemma. She had to learn to listen to her inner feelings, what she felt was best for herself, not what or her mother or her neighbors or I might think. She learned to work through her dreams in which various parts of herself began revealing her innermost feelings. Finally she learned that she had resources within herself to make decisions and change her life.

RESOURCES

In moving out into unknown worlds and in developing a sense of self, we need special spiritual attributes. Against the lion of the loss of support and the fear of falling, we need the shield of trust and faith. It takes time to grow psychological eyes and ears, to learn that we can trust and act on our perceptions. This slow process means taking one step, one day, one new effort, and one new activity at a time. Unbinding spiritual feet to walk alone takes an infinite amount of patience.

Against the tiger of the fear of confusion and lack of self-control, we need the shield of will. This is about the flabbiest muscle I ever had to develop. I've had to grit my teeth and move on even when I didn't want to. I had to find all sorts of ways to reward my self for doing so. Sometimes it would have been easier to stay in bed and sleep; many times it would have been easier to say no to myself and stay trapped in my Me shell. Finally my alternatives were reduced either to suffocating to death or kicking myself into action. Learning to exercise the will requires incentive, goal and direction, something to move toward in the future—even if in the beginning it's just to escape slow death another way.

The defense we have against the bears of separation anxiety and the fear of being alone is the power of a sense of purpose and meaning, something we would be *willing* to *die* for or, what is sometimes even harder, something we'd be *willing* to *live* for. The child willing to practice an hour a day to learn to play a musical instrument has the goal of wanting to play as well as the teacher. The woman *willing* to be herself often needs a role-model, a woman she admires and wants to be like. One woman with whom I talked had a deathly fear of speaking in committees and public meetings. However, she respected the former president of her club very much, and so the first time she had to preside over a meeting, she pretended to be the other woman. It worked. She learned that she could speak up and take charge—of both her timid self and the business of the meeting. It was a good feeling, she said, an exhilarating sense of finding herself capable of something new.

If you have difficulty visualizing yourself changing in any way or trying new activities and new ways of behaving, perhaps you can use your imagination and think of a woman you could emulate. When I was sixteen and learning to fly an airplane, my heroine was Amelia

Earhart; later on when I was thinking of going back to school, my role-model was another woman who had done so with five children. But pick your role-model carefully and realistically. For example, I didn't know that my role-model had her mother nearby to baby sit for her and that she had been a magna cum laude student!

Such a role-model may be an idealized self-image, a woman who has already developed capabilities within herself which are still potential and latent within you. Make a list of five characteristics you admire in your role-model and begin to exercise those attributes as your personal goals. Following a person serves as a new focus when we journey along a foggy route into the unknown.

Trust (faith), will, and purpose are the shields we can carry with us as we move into the forest of the self toward the goal of personal *I*dentity. By actualizing these resources we acquire basic attitudes to use in whatever personal projects lie ahead.

CHAPTER 5

Self-Discovery

Every week my Sunday newspaper offers a travel section jampacked with advertisements and articles describing trips for rest and relaxation or to see new scenery or to discover other peoples and their different ways of life. All it takes is time, money, and the desire to pick oneself up and move away from familiar surroundings for a while. A trip like that, whether it's for ten thousand or one thousand miles, begins with a single step into the unknown.

The journey toward self-discovery begins differently. Basically it has to be a do-it-yourself trip. It needn't take any money or time away from your usual activities or routines. You can do it right where you live with all the people and in all the places you know. It needn't take you away from your job or your loved ones.

It does require a difference in your attitude. You must be willing to risk discovering something new about yourself and your relationships with other people. This sounds simple, but it demands a shift in the way you perceive yourself: You are a unique, separate individual, different in a special way from every other person. You have your own constellation of talents and attributes. You see, feel, and sense things differently from day to day than anybody else. You can make choices each day you live that will affect people around you positively or negatively.

How can you separate yourself from those around you and discover your uniqueness? First, there are inner tasks, the things you do internally which will affect the way you look at things and make choices. This inner dimension influences your outer tasks, the things you do related to the people with whom you live and work.

Participating in this process will result in a transformation of your self-image. On the surface nothing much will seem to change, but the way you perceive the totality of life will be different. It's like an optical illusion, a sketch that appears to be a tall goblet but from a different perspective looks like two facing profiles. In other words, nothing changes but the way you look at things, out of your own center instead of through others' eyes.

SEPARATING: A THIN LINE OF DIFFERENCE

Sometimes it's hard to think of ourselves as different from anybody else; so the first step in learning to separate is to conceptualize the difference between yourself and every other person. To get an idea of how to begin the process, try this experiment. On a piece of paper (recycle an envelop from the wastebasket if you'd like to save a tree!), draw a line anywhere you want it. Label the space on one side of the line YOU, the other side, ME. Please take the time to do this before reading ahead.

Now what kind of line did you draw? A straight line? From top to bottom or just part way? A curve or a diagonal? Or a wavy Mississippi River replica? Oh, did you presume I meant a straight line? No, all I said was a line.

The next thing I'm interested in is how much space you gave YOU on the paper. Did ME and YOU get equal space, or did you give most of the space to YOU and keep only a little for ME, or vice versa?

This simple visual aid is not a gimmick, but it can reveal a great deal about your self-perception. The line that divides ME from YOU describes your psychological territory in several ways. If you allotted the biggest portion of the paper to YOU, you might want to ask yourself how much space and time you allow yourself from day to day. Do you just keep giving and giving like Mother Earth or Red Cross Nurse and never take anything for yourself? Do you give all the speaking time to others or do you do all the talking? And do you feel continually put upon because nobody does anything for you?

Most women unconsciously wipe out the thin line of difference between themselves and other people, or if they draw it at all, they give away most of the paper to the YOU side and don't keep anything for themselves. They manage to give away all their time and space to others. It's not that they are just being passive and letting other people walk over them. They assume they're being unselfish in always letting another person have first choice. It's as though they haven't learned the difference between themselves and others. I can unconsciously give all my time to others and then wonder why I have a headache, why I am so tired or hungry.

One of my hardest tasks over the past few years has been to question how much I've been giving myself away to other people—either assuming they'd reciprocate or that it just didn't make any difference because "we're all one." We aren't all one. Each of us is unique and different. It's risky to say that, but it's beautiful to know it.

Another thing I do that reflects my not having drawn that imaginary thin line of difference between YOU and ME is that I assume I know what you are thinking or feeling and that you know what I'm thinking or feeling. Somehow we keep taking for granted that people know what we mean and that we know what other people mean. Most TV situation comedies are based on misunderstandings that occur because of this mixed-up kind of thinking. One person assumes she knows what the other person is going to do or say—which turns out to be the wrong thing. It was funny when Lucille Ball played those roles, but it's not so funny in real life.

It took a very dramatic experience for me to realize how much I tended to ignore the boundary lines of my existence and accommodate the other person. A few years ago I was at a workshop for professionals interested in body talk and body language. Because not enough women had volunteered, I wound up taking part while others watched from the sidelines. In one of the first demonstrations the leader went around the circle of twelve, one by one, pressing his index fingers into a special point along the upper side of our jaw lines. I couldn't imagine what was going on. When he finally reached me, he looked into my eyes, asking my permission to begin. I nodded. At first the pressure was all right, but then I began to feel uncomfortable. I suppose I frowned, but he didn't stop. He just kept pressing on the bone, harder and harder. Suddenly I reached my threshold of pain, and I reacted. I was hurt and mad. How dare he? He was violating the boundary of what I could and would accept; he was trespassing. I was really angry and knocked his hands away. What he'd done wasn't fair. Later I realized he would have kept up the pressure until I drew the line. He was waiting for me to realize who I was and what was mine alone. He proved something to me I'll never forget. Each of us has to learn to draw the thin line of difference between our *selves* and others and to respect that difference.

Saying this seems elementary, and obvious, but I still find myself repeatedly assuming I know what another person is thinking or feeling, and I find other people assuming the same about me. I constantly have to keep checking and rechecking what belongs on each side of the line: which is ME and which is YOU. At this point the inner and outer tasks become vitally important.

INNER TASKS

Sorting out who you are as a unique person will probably turn out to be a lifetime task. But beginning, like writing the first sentence of a book or a term paper, is often one of the most difficult parts. How do we start getting in touch with our selves, recognizing our talents and attributes, becoming responsible for our choices and actions? Somehow we have to find our centers and keep in touch with them despite outside pressures that tug and pull from every direction.

But, more often than not, many women begin this process involuntarily. For each woman I've met who consciously decided to set out on the path of self-development, I've met two others who were forced into it. Sometimes I think that what has been called "women's liberation" is just one part of a greater movement which would better be termed "women's survival."

Matilda and her "sisters"—Mona, Marcia, Maybelle, Miriam, and Maxine—represent women who have been thrown into the process of self-discovery in order to survive. Each was forced into discovering themselves by a variety of outside circumstances. Mona's children had outgrown their need for her Earth Motherhood. Marcia's husband had been too immature to stay in any marriage. Maybelle's husband was a perennial adolescent, the philandering type who used her more as a mother than a wife. Marianne's husband left her because he couldn't bear her clinging. Miriam had never quite left her mother's apron strings and was searching for a man to take her mother's place.

Working with these women was difficult because each began by transferring her dependency needs on me. Each had been shocked by external factors into having to outgrow the Me stage; each presumed that somebody on the outside could do her work for her. Slowly we had to examine from the inside out who each was as an individual, what she wanted for herself, and how she could best set goals and make choices.

Marianne Johnson (see chap. 1, p. 18) had been exceptionally sheltered. She had been the typical happy homemaker, the kind who flies to the door to greet husband George just like the popular song that enjoins women "to make him your reason for living." She wrapped herself around his every word, smothering him with attention. She wasn't just living through him; in a symbiotic sense she *was* him. She had worked as an office clerk to put him through college, but she had hated every minute of her job. She was working only for him-her. As soon as he graduated, she collapsed within the four walls of their apartment, depending completely and permanently on him for all life's goodies. "Let George do it" was her theme song. If I had asked her to draw a diagram of her life back then, it would have been a circle enclosing YOU-ME.

But George grew tired of the arrangement. When he was in school and she worked, she'd at least had her job to consume some time and energy. When she quit, everything landed on his shoulders, and he objected. He wanted a child, but she wasn't ready. She wanted to save up a bit more money first and buy all the things she needed for her cozy little nest. Actually she hadn't been ready for motherhood because she was still a dependent child herself.

When George rebelled, he really rebelled. One week everything had apparently been great; the next he moved out, taking his clothes and belongings. All he left behind was their joint checking account and his verbal promise (since he wanted to be a gentleman) to deposit enough money monthly for Marianne to buy groceries and pay the rent.

Marianne was devastated. Her world had been shattered. She felt she had nothing left to live for. She might have committed suicide— but she was afraid of failing and being hospitalized. Somehow she hung on, week after week, wondering what she'd done wrong, trying every ploy she could think of to get George back. He had been the center of her life; without him, she drifted, waiting for a miracle to bring him back.

Slowly, after several months, she began to take some responsibility for herself—out of sheer necessity at first. Some things she had to do —pay the bills, decide whether or not to renew the lease on their apartment (she did), choose new paint as part of the renewal. Her biggest hurdle was finding a job. George threatened to stop sending money after six months; so she really couldn't delay. But week after week she came in, saying she'd bought the Sunday paper and hadn't seen any jobs that appealed to her. The fact was she was afraid to find one and have to call for an interview. Finally she got up enough courage to try an indirect approach—an employment agency. She had developed some office skills in the job she'd had before; so she did find work as a Gal Friday in a one-man office. Her first paycheck was a milestone. Reluctantly, unwillingly, she told me one day that she was glad to be working again. Dating, however, was another problem that took months to work through. In the beginning Marianne fell desperately in love on the first date with any man who seemed like George.

She was looking for someone to take her under his wing and adopt her. Fortunately none of the men she met wanted that kind of arrangement; gradually she began to sort out for herself the kind of man with whom she might build a new life.

After over a year and a half Marianne was able to separate herself from George and begin establishing her own identity. It was hard work right from the start because embarking on the journey of self-discovery had not been her choice. Slowly she realized that in learning to stand on her own and support herself she had achieved something no one could ever take away.

Although Marianne's process began against her will, some women awaken spontaneously and wonder who they are. A number of young wives and mothers have told me that one day they just began questioning what they were doing and if that was all there was to life. Often this awakening came after their youngest child was a few years old and they knew that having another child was more than they could handle. The spell of motherhood and romantic love had vanished, and they were face-to-face with themselves at last.

Sarah Moore's path led in that direction. For several years before she came to see me, she had been an invisible woman, immersed in wife- and motherhood. The death of a close friend had shocked her into awareness. Depressed and in mourning, she began to withdraw the projections of herself which had been running out into the world through her three children and husband. In a psychic low, she felt spurts of energy from the women's movement but couldn't seem to get going.

Mostly she was angry about the years she'd wasted, wished she'd been doing more with her life, wished she hadn't married the first nice guy who'd come along, wished that she hadn't had children year after year, one right after another. And she felt guilty about those feelings. She loved her children and her husband. She knew they weren't to blame; so she blamed herself. Round and round she went: numb, withdrawn, angry, guilty. She wanted to do something for herself, but she didn't know how. She was stuck.

Then she slowly began to move and grow, but unevenly as is typical.

For example, recently she came to see me on the verge of tears. For the past several months she had made great progress getting in touch with herself and setting goals. She was singing in a choral group for the first time since high school. She was exchanging child-sitting with a neighbor so she could take tailoring lessons at a special sewing clinic. She enrolled in a college preparation equivalency course.

But then she'd gotten herself wiped out by a combination of typical circumstances: her husband was out of town on a business trip; her three children had the intestinal flu, so she couldn't ask her neighbor to watch them, and had to miss class. She had retreated to her bedroom in tears, defeated. All the weeks of work seemed wiped out. She wasn't angry or bitter, just blank and empty. All the outside world seemed to be against her growth, and she was giving up. It just didn't seem worth the extra hassles. What difference would it make if she ever went back to school?

What Sarah needed more than anything else right then was to get back in touch with her selfhood. She didn't need to talk much; what she'd told me was enough. Right then she didn't need questions or supportive listening from me. All I could do was honor her need to find herself; so we did something we'd never done before in a session.

First, I asked her to ground herself in her chair, to get both her feet on the floor, and to rest her arms comfortably in her lap. Next, I asked her to close her eyes and listen to the sounds outside herself. I did likewise; so I'd be in touch with the process. It was amazing how much we heard—airplanes flying by, children laughing and squealing in the distance, a few birds chirping, trucks and cars passing by, telephones ringing in the distance. When Sarah and I were talking, I hadn't heard any of those things. What we were doing was getting back in touch with our senses, getting back into our selves. Too much of the time we are "sense"-less, out of hearing, smelling, feeling, tasting.

Next I asked Sarah to pay attention to her breathing, to count her breaths in and out without changing the rhythm. I did the same. Just as we don't listen to sounds around us, so often we block out awareness of our bodies. Getting in touch with our breathing is another way of recovering our sense of wholeness and integrity. I also asked Sarah if she could feel her pulse or heartbeat.

After we'd been breathing in and out slowly for a while, I asked Sarah to breathe more deeply, to fill her lungs more fully. I was asking her to expand her sense of responsibility for her selfhood. Too often I blank out everything about myself by focusing outside on other things and other people. I need to keep my *self* in better balance. Deep breathing seems to help me, and in this case it worked for Sarah.

A few minutes later we both opened our eyes. Sarah let out a big sigh, blinked her eyes a bit, and said, "I feel much better." She had gotten some space for herself. She was ready to talk about what had been happening so that she could see how to deal with the circumstances instead of being overwhelmed by them. She was ready to see how she had retreated into her old childlike passivity, giving up her dreams for self. She didn't want to feel that she would always continue to sacrifice herself for others; she was tired of that and angry at herself for falling into earlier behavior patterns.

Over several months Sarah had made real gains which needn't have been wiped out or ignored. It was time for her to see how some outside pressures she had been feeling were really pressures of her own, feelings from inside she had put on herself. Her expectations for herself had been high. Her self-criticism was more intense than her husband's or neighbors' could have been. She was getting ready for the next step of looking at the other side of that thin line between YOU and ME.

OUTSIDE TASKS

We can almost mark off as stepping-stones the various feelings we have toward others and ourselves as we move through the Myself stage. In general we move from the Me stage with its passive apathy toward our selves into the free-wheeling I stage of selfhood and autonomy. In between we feel anxious and guilty about separating from others, angry toward others, and depressed (which can be anger turned inward toward ourselves). As we begin to get more in touch with our true centers, these feelings are all mixed up. From week to week our moods fluctuate. One week we're on top of the world because we have a sense of being able to achieve things for ourselves. The next week we're thrown back because the world isn't out there awaiting us with open arms. Growing and moving toward independence hurts. It's painful to bump up against other people who don't seem ready for our change.

In working with other people, however, one of our hardest tasks is to sort out the real feelings other people have toward us and those we think they have. During the Me stage we identified with other people. As we become unique individuals, we recognize that other people are also unique. They are not always going to agree with us, and we must learn to live with and tolerate individual differences. As we gain more space for ourselves, we're faced with learning how to check out other persons and find out where they are coming from. We learn to allow them space also.

The sequence goes something like this: In the Me stage I assume that you and I are exactly the same, that I know what you are thinking and you know what I am thinking. We are the same; so we must do, think, and feel exactly the same. We cannot tolerate individual differences because that threatens to separate us, and we don't dare stand alone.

These patterns begin in early childhood and continue into adult life. If a mother constantly says to her child, "That's not the way *we* do things," the child gives up daring to try doing anything new. Or, if a mother says, "Don't make me angry!" the child learns that anger means separation and loss of love.

In the Myself stage we begin to suspect that we are different. We begin to draw that thin line of difference between our selves and others. We begin to need space and time alone. First, we're afraid that our growth might upset people we love or work with, and so we begin to draw back into ourselves and get depressed. Next we begin to resent what we assume others are thinking and feeling about us, and we get angry with them because we think they are resisting our growth.

During this stage we may find that our feelings shift dramatically. Instead of feeling anxious or guilty, we may feel depressed and/or angry. There are many types of depression, but this kind is really anger we turn back against ourselves. In doing so we block our growth. We dare not move directly toward other people who we think might not want us to grow. We hold our feelings and thoughts inside. We fail to check out our feelings and perceptions with others because we are afraid they might get angry with us and we might lose their love.

Mary Harris exemplified this dilemma. In one way she was like Marianne; she overidentified with her husband, Jim, and didn't want anything to separate them and change their idyllic honeymoon pattern of perfect we-ness. But in another way she was like Sarah. She wanted to grow and be independent as she had been before her marriage. She kept these feelings bottled up inside herself. She never told Jim what she felt about their plans. She always deferred to him, not wanting to indicate contrary opinions. Inside, however, she became angrier and angrier, but all that showed was depression. She began to make sniping, hostile comments about Jim, criticizing him in front of their friends because he never did anything she wanted. She kept thinking he could read her mind, and of course he couldn't.

At the same time, Jim was getting angry at her. He hated her dependence upon him. He felt she wanted him to make all the decisions. He wanted to know what she was thinking and feeling. He said he spent hours questioning her about what was wrong between them, but she would only cry and want him to guess what was wrong. By the time he found out, he was too tired and no longer cared. He was really angry at her but couldn't tell her so directly. He wanted a fuller relationship with her but didn't know how to break through the barrier of silence. They began drifting apart, and he started to look for someone else with whom he could really talk and have a little fun. Mary had turned into a silent grouch.

What was wrong was that old cliché from the movie *Cool Hand Luke:* "What we have here is a failure to communicate." Jim and Mary's marriage began blowing apart because neither could tell the other directly what he or she was thinking and feeling. Mary was depressed; Jim was angry. They were two different people with two different sets of needs and wants. Both required time and space for themselves but kept trying to pretend they were still "one" from their honeymoon days. The illusion of romantic love faded as they began to outgrow that inadequate base. They needed a more mature form of love. Unfortunately Jim began to look outside the marriage instead of working through his communication gap with Mary.

During the Myself period we need to work through two communication tasks: First, we have to practice acknowledging directly what we think and feel. We have to own (perceive or recognize) our thoughts and emotions so we can tell others in simple terms what's going on inside us. We have to provide facts about our feelings and opinions so that others can make decisions based upon accurate information. For example, suppose you and a friend or loved one had been planning to go to a movie on Friday night, but you are too tired. All the other person needs to hear is something like this: "I'm really too tired tonight to go out to a movie. I'd like to be able to keep you company, but it's just not a movie I want to see that much. I wouldn't mind if you went alone and I just stayed home and washed my hair."

Second, we have to check out what the other person is feeling and thinking. We can make direct statements expressing our need to know. For example:

"I really would like to know what you meant."

"I get the feeling you're bothered by what I said."

"I don't know what's going on with you. Would you tell me, please?"

The more we begin to communicate directly and check out what others are feeling, the more we begin to appreciate the natural, normal differences that exist between us. Such differences don't need to change the way we love each other. In fact, the more we learn about each other's differences, the more we can celebrate them and share with each other—and the more we can feel free to become ourselves.

I and Identity

The Myself stage is a period of transition and development, a time of searching and changing, as we discover our selves for the first time. The I stage is new territory in which our horizons expand and we gain a clear sense of who we are and where we're going. This is a centered sort of time when we feel our identity and recognize our personal capabilities. This stage would normally occur toward the end of adolescence, but, whenever we get there, it is a time of fulfillment and hope.

In one way, the I stage is a time of special challenge and growth. New conflicts and tensions appear. In our work it's a time for developing competence as well as dealing with competition and authority. In personal relationships it is a time for the possibility of intimacy based upon reciprocal sharing and caring between equally independent persons.

CHAPTER 6

One Is One!

How will you know when you've arrived at the I stage? Can you look forward to some special day you will be able to mark off on the calendar? Is it like graduation or the day you got promoted at the office or the day you lost your virginity? Is there some particular ceremony or rite of transition you can celebrate?

The questions are fair, but the answers are frustrating. No, the I stage can't be marked off like arriving at the destination after a long trip. No, you'll probably never know exactly which day you've finally made it. No, there isn't any particular way you can celebrate.

The I stage isn't a goal you get to but a way of being in the world. Getting there is more a result of practicing than suddenly arriving. It's more like finally learning to hit your stride in a skill—riding a two-wheeler, skiing, playing the violin, making an especially flaky pie-crust, getting an article published, being able to charge for work you've done well. You can't see, eat, smell, or taste the I stage, but you can be in it and enjoy it.

Each of us has a certain particular potential for being or becoming which we can practice and then draw on when necessary. I get frustrated at one of the distinctions routinely given to describe the difference between men and women: Men *do;* women *are.* Nonsense. What we are cannot be separated from what we do. We need to be doing that which is a part of our becoming.

On several occasions I've had to use the word *I* to get across what I was thinking and feeling in a crucial situation. One time I was having to lay down some limits for one of my daughters. She was seventeen, behaving obnoxiously, and we both knew it. She didn't like what I said at all and was testing me on an issue. She wanted to take advantage of my so-called maternal compassion and was trying to con me into letting her have the car after she'd broken a rule we'd agreed upon.

When I spoke, I finally cut the last remnants of the psychological umbilical cord which had bound us. I don't remember the precise words; specifically they weren't that important. What counted was the emotion and the certainty out of which I spoke: "Look, kiddo. I don't care if you don't like what I'm saying, but this rule has to stick, period." Over the next few years we had to work through more things between us as she established her identity. But that episode established my identity in terms of my own personhood. I finally stopped placating her in the hopes she would behave better on the basis that we were both the same. In a way it was a weaning, and it drew a clear line of difference between us.

Other times when I have been able to speak out of my center have been equally important. One milestone occurred during my divorce trial; I had to defend my rights against my former husband's lawyer. The man was arguing that I didn't need financial support while I finished my graduate degree. He thought I could just go to work and support myself entirely. His client didn't have to pay. Somewhere out of my depths I found myself saying, "Look, man. If you were in your senior year at law school, and someone told you to drop out and go to work, would you do it?" He, of course, said no and backed down. Once again I had been able to assert my rights responsibly and confront an authority outside myself. I'd called up that steel inside myself which my lawyer had told me I'd need.

What do you feel like when you get into the I stage? Are there marks of distinction that set this stage off from the others? Are there particular exercises you can practice?

Technically speaking, the I stage is a period of psychological equilibrium in which a person establishes *ego identity.* In other words, it is that key portion of human development during which we combine many things, such as a sense of autonomy and the ability to take initiative, being active instead of passive, and working through conflicts between internal and external demands.

Over the years I've heard many women describe how they discovered this sense of themselves. Their experiences were different, but their transitional points illustrate the same dynamics. One group of professional women and homemakers working part-time to establish competence in crafts and the arts found great pleasure sharing details of their growth.

Sally Winters, a member of that group, had just begun succeeding as a free-lance photographer. She explained that her special moment of transition occurred when she decided she would have to begin developing her prints. At that point she gained control over the quality of her pictures, and began to be aware of more factors when she took them. Jane Wilson, on the other hand, runs her own pottery business out of a shop in her basement. She crossed that line of awareness when she realized she would have to decide for herself whether to mass produce several of her original designs or continue to experiment creatively and produce only a limited quantity of each one. It was a difficult decision because it would drastically affect her regular income. A free-lance writer, Joanne Webster, described how she had to research the historical backgrounds of her characters, a task which led her away from her dining-room-table office out into the world. This decision grew out of her desire for professional integrity and authenticity. It not only enriched her material but meant that she began meeting new people.

Sally, Jane, and Joanne are examples of how we develop individually as we get in touch with ourselves. In the process we may feel very much alone as we try to maintain a balance between family demands and professional growth needs, but making decisions leads into new self-awareness in relation to our skills. In general I would sum up these awarenesses as follows:

Establishing a sense of separateness as part of our work. As we begin to follow a line of interest within a particular field of work, we must acquire emotional independence so that we have space and time for ourselves. This means finding time for our work, which can be particularly difficult if the job is done at home, such as writing, photography, and pottery. It's one thing to separate yourself from the family if you can leave for the office at a regular time each day; it's another thing if the children are around making demands. Traditionally men have not had to deal with this particular phenomenon. Their right to "a room of one's own" (both psychological and physical) was taken for granted. Not so for women. Perhaps one reason married women with families go into volunteer work or back to school is to pick up on that lost sense of work and reestablish it in combination with family life. We need that healthy balance in order to keep our work our work and our love our love. As more women decide not to have children or to have just a few, it is crucial to be able to find ways of realizing creativity and responsibility through individual work.

Establishing a new way of relating emotionally to other people. As we give up former dependent patterns (typical of the Me stage), we begin to find individual strength and no longer need to lean on others emotionally. This doesn't mean, however, that we have to give up warm emotional sharing with others which involves mutuality and caring. It just means that we stand in our own space on our own ground as our own person. We then find our times with other people enriched as we share our new experiences and they share with us. In our work fields meet others who share the common interests which come with doing the same work. The word which means this sort of sharing is *collegiality,* and I use it to stand for a special kind of comradeship and camaraderie which is hard to describe. Several times after particularly deep, rewarding experiences as one of a team of leaders in a participative group leadership training program I went back to my room and cried because I couldn't find that sort of relationship with my husband. What I experienced was a team of persons, each competent in his or her own way, sharing insights and perspectives in a process of consultation in which no one had to be defensive or competitive. It was a rare, exhilarating, heady experience that I wish more people could know.

Getting to be good at doing something. I can't begin to describe the good feelings I get when I see the marvelously competent work women are beginning to achieve. This is a sort of objective, admiration for work well done, and it can come in a number of ways at home and at work. I wrote a poem for my friend Jane, the potter, after a dinner party she had given which was outstanding for its overall ambience. I knew the hours of preparation it took her to achieve the flow between people as they enjoyed her easy hospitality and the delicious food. I admire other women for the sweaters they knit, the needlecraft they design, the excellent meetings they conduct, the beautiful, orderly homes they keep (an ability I don't have). I admire competence and beauty, and I hate the way some women downgrade themselves and shrug off compliments instead of being able to accept them graciously.

The process of getting to be good at whatever we choose requires that we recognize realistically our positive and negative characteristics. We must not only be able to accept objective criticism from others, but also be able to critique our own work. For me this means being able to write something, and then rewrite it, and then rewrite again and again and again. I have to get a certain amount of objective space between myself and my work so that I don't overidentify with it—as I used to do with my children. Sociologists call this sort of objectivity *role-distance.* Emotionally we are ourselves as persons; our work is our work, a separate entity.

Living out of our centers as persons, distinct from both our work and our loves. It's difficult to distinguish between our internal qualities as persons with unique capabilities and feelings and our outer shells, façades or social identities in relation to other people. One might compare this shift in attitude about ourselves to the difference between a *clear* fluid and a lovely colored one (green, amber, gold, or whatever). The clear fluid can be poured into any number of different colored glass vases and apparently take on the color of the vase. The colored one can be poured into any number of differently shaped clear containers and illuminate each of them.

Our inner color, our vibration, our personhood, is our inner identity regardless of what we do or with whom we do it. It involves keeping enough psychological distance from our work to be able to live without it. It means that we can take the personal skills needed in one job and transfer them to other fields. Career management people stress that we each have unique emotional factors and skills which transcend any one particular job. For example, a teacher who is good at detail can transfer that skill into another career which requires detail work. Women who have acquired interpersonal skills in working with others in volunteer activities can use those skills to advantage in personnel work. I love a line in the television movie *Tell Me Where It Hurts.* Maureen Stapleton told her husband that she'd gotten her job because as an older woman she had a skill younger women don't have: patience.

Setting goals and working toward them. If there is any one attribute I would wish to give a woman just setting out to find herself both in work and love, it would be perseverance. I know how long it took to get my graduate degree and how many obstacles seemed to get in my way, but at birth (yes, I'm a Taurus) someone must have given me perseverance. The first thing women need to do is set goals for themselves and then keep focused on those instead of on the obstacles.

Sylvia West had become depressed because her husband Philip traveled a great deal. She always seemed to be home alone with their four children, so she volunteered to dance in a local hospital benefit show. She felt good, getting out at night and making new friends. But gradually, she became discouraged over the difficulty finding sitters for late night rehearsals. She considered quitting the show because she lost track of her goal. She had to stretch in order to juggle her new time schedule. She hung on—deciding the new frustrations were better than the old.

Now that we've seen what the I stage is like, we can look more carefully into its various dynamics and a few of the specific emotional tasks involved in developing ego-strengths.

CHAPTER 7

Portrait of Yourself

I'd like you to draw a portrait of yourself. You don't have to be an artist to do it. You don't need special paper or paints unless you'd like to turn this into an original abstract to hang over the fireplace. You can do it on a scrap of paper retrieved from the wastebasket or on a blank page inside the cover of this book. You also need some colored pencils or crayons.

What I'd like you to do is scribble the way children do for fun in kindergarten. Draw a long curving line that loops around, back and forth, up and down, crisscrossing all over the place and making all sorts of little nooks and crannies.

After you've drawn the scribble, begin to differentiate separate areas within it. First, pick out an inner shape, not quite in the middle, which is interesting or pleasing to you. This is part 1. Set it off by going over its edges and making it darker. Fill it in with your favorite color. Now pick out an area adjacent to part 1 which encloses or overlaps it in some way, and fill it in with another color. This is part 2.

The third step is to go all around the edges of the scribble with a darker line so that it will stand out dramatically from the rest of the page. We'll call this outer line part 3.

The last step at this time is to draw two lines which will enclose the whole scribble: first, a dotted line, 4A, which goes all around smoothing off the rough edges, and then a final darker line, 4B, which encloses the whole form.

Once I asked a group of women I'd known for years to draw this scribble during a discussion group. Their anxiety level got so high they spent fifteen minutes asking how I wanted them to do it. Each one apparently thought she might reveal herself significantly—as one might do on a special psychological test. That's not the purpose of our scribble-portrait; it's just a device to explain various aspects of our conscious and unconscious.

Part 1 symbolizes your present area of consciousness, and you can put a big black dot in the middle of it to represent the ego as its center.

Part 2 represents your preconscious. It contains the material which potentially can become conscious: experiences, facts you've known and forgotten, dreams you've hoped to make come true, anything you could retrieve from your memory bank if asked key questions such as, What's the first memory you have of your mother? Who was your favorite elementary school teacher?

Part 3, the outer line, represents the boundaries of your essential personhood, everything that makes you different from everybody else. This line is your uniqueness and contains your potential integrity. It's the outer edge between the real limits of you and the rest of the world, the limits of your perceptions, experiences, and unconscious.

Line 4A represents our social selves, the way we smooth ourselves off in order to present ourselves to the world, the way our parents taught us to live in their society. It is dotted because most of the time there is an appropriate boundary between ourselves and others; we don't have to let everything hang out. We can use *selective authenticity;* we can moderate what we say and do.

The darker heavier line, 4B, is a defensive shield we may have developed as a protective device. Such a shield, however, boxes us in, inhibits us, restricts our movement. It is a heavy façade behind which we hide from others. Persons with shields like this aren't quite real; they're elusive, stiff, rigid, cool, contained, opaque, difficult to communicate with and hard to relate to. They may put up a good social front and appear to be making it, but I often wonder where the person is who lives inside. It's important to remember, however, that the shell is there for a reason—to protect something which needs protecting, more often than not a fragile self, an undeveloped self which may never have been encouraged to grow.

Now we'll turn to the way the ego functions within our selfhood, but don't throw away the scribble. We'll come back to it in chapter 9.

UNDERSTANDING THE EGO

It's difficult to describe the ego without using all sorts of images and metaphors. Whatever device I use only points to how the ego works, which is still basically a mystery. Freud originally described the ego as the inner agency within the mind which mediated between the powerful instinctual drives of the body (the id) and the social conditioning or the patterns we internalized as children from parents and society (the superego). He considered the ego weak and defensive, but today ego psychologists see it as a powerful internal agency which mediates all our inner and outer needs and synthezies our various selves—body, social, cognitive, idealized images of ourself, and so on. On the inside the ego deals with the power of the instincts, feelings, emotions, and perceptions. On the outside it keeps us in touch with the physical reality of our environment and with the social reality of interpersonal relationships. The ego learns to balance these forces and needs.

Much like an iceberg floats in the water, the ego floats in the unconscious; it is both conscious and unconscious. We may become more conscious of the ego's tasks, which strengthens it in the process, but we can never become entirely aware of all the ego is—nor can we know the pervasiveness of its strength once developed.

According to the ego psychologist Erik H. Erikson, there are eight different stages in our lives during which we work through specific crises which lead toward our acquiring specific ego strengths or virtues. In infancy the crisis is between basic trust and basic mistrust, and

the ego strength the baby gains is hope. In early childhood the conflicts are autonomy versus shame and self-doubt, leading to will, and
initiative versus guilt, leading to purpose. Early school years present
the crisis between industry and inferiority, hopefully leading to competence. During adolescence, the crisis between identity and identity
confusion and role diffusion leads both toward faith and toward sufficient ego identity which makes possible the next two stages of adult
life: intimacy versus isolation, with love; generativity versus stagna-
tion, with care. In our later years we face death, and the crisis of
integrity versus despair presents us with the possibility of gaining
wisdom.

Each stage is related to the next. At each new crisis we have the
challenge and potentiality of not only developing new skills but of
reworking previous tasks which were incompleted because of insuffi-
cient social support, tensions beyond our control, or external crises.
This is how a woman who has failed to find her identity during the
fifth stage (adolescence) is really pushed during the seventh crisis
toward developing a form of caring which will extend beyond her
nuclear family in order to serve both the needs of her underdeveloped
self and the wider needs of the world.

In terms of attaining these various ego strengths, women have been
short-changed. For many reasons, some of which we've already dis-
cussed, they have been unable to develop several of these basic capacities. How much basic trust do you have that the world will accept you
as a woman? Can you take initiative and do something new, taking
responsibility, feeling competent, realizing your own autonomy?
Women often come out better in the loving, caring half of life, but
that's because these ego strengths come out of fulfilling the rule assigned in adolescence of being a "good woman" and of being rewarded
socially for these attributes. It seems as though only in old age are
women forced to face the crisis of being alone and finding themselves.
Only then, as widows with "empty nests," when it is a matter of sheer
survival, do many women begin to meet the crises of autonomy and
initiative. Maybe that's why older persons seem difficult; their wills
conflict with the wills of people around them. In senescence they are
still working through basic issues of childhood and adolescence.

THE ABC'S OF EGO-STRENGTH

The woman stuck in the Me stage has been unable to gain the ego strengths needed to progress normally through life. Because of her weak ego, she hides behind the shell of an outside role, depending on others, being what she thinks they want her to be. She is exceptionally vulnerable to the powerful forces of romantic love and motherhood. She is also not in touch with the undeveloped aspects of her masculine side and does not know how to deal with so-called male problems because she has never developed the required ego strengths. She is ignorant of the simple ABC tasks for working in the world.

During the I state, therefore, we need to work through specific problem areas that have to do with strengths instead of weaknesses. We have to face and learn to use anger, aggression, assertion, the balance of power, conflict, competition, and success. This takes a strong ego.

From Apathy, Anger, and Aggression to Appropriate Assertion and Authority. Recently many popular books in the field of psychology have dealt with assertion and women. Basically these books take a behavioristic approach to the problems of learning to assert ourselves without feeling guilty. They provide specific exercises for dealing with situations in which we are apt to give away power over ourselves to other people. They provide models for ways in which we can effectively make our needs and wants known.

From the standpoint of ego development, these books are helping women work through unresolved crises from the second and third life-stages. They face head-on basic questions of how we can realize our autonomy and exercise our initiative. It appears that there is no good reason adults should have to say yes when they want to say no, or why they should feel guilty.

It seems incredible that adult women should retreat from asserting themselves appropriately; yet we do. In part, anxiety keeps us from asserting ourselves, and this stems from inability to draw the thin line of difference between ourselves and others. If we aren't different and if we don't stand up for ourselves, we don't have to work through separation anxiety, and we can stay in a comfortable symbiosis with the other person. This sort of anxiety gets mixed up in a circular pattern with feelings of inadequacy and insecurity. If we never risk growing, our muscles of autonomy and initiative remain unexercised, and we are actually inadequate. We have to practice and grow one step at a time out of old patterns.

We also refuse to assert ourselves because of the secondary gains we can make by not being in charge. Sometimes it's easier to look back at how we got the way we are than to see what we are still getting out of staying on one level of development. We can get insight into the past, we can do all sorts of exercises which provide us with ways to be more firm and assertive, but it's harder to see what the pay-off may be for not taking that last step over the boundary line from dependency into independence and autonomy. What keeps women from wanting to be in authority? from wanting to move ahead? What inner mechanism keeps us happy to be first vice-president and executive secretary instead of president and executive director? What keeps us from wanting to be where the buck finally does stop? What keeps us out of that executive kitchen where the heat is? Is it that we can't take the heat? that we're afraid of being alone and of losing love? that we might succeed?

The answers to these questions are complex. First, I think we get scared and back off from authority and assertion because we fear feeling alone. We're afraid of getting angry because we have repressed anger so long. We don't know how to deal with it appropriately in bits and pieces; we have commonly held it in as long as possible and then let it all out at once in a big explosion. Part of the problem also comes from our childhood, from mistakes our parents made but also from our unconscious overidentification with past authority figures. We fear becoming like those who hurt us and restrained us as children. In *The Pedagogy of the Oppressed,* Paulo Friere explains that all too often oppressed persons have had no role-models other than the oppressor. When the oppressed finally fight their way to independence, their only known ways of behaving are like those who had controlled them—and so they repeat the oppression. Men fear women's gaining power because of their own unresolved Oedipal problems; a woman in charge might repeat the same oppression they knew as young boys. Women fear taking charge because it might mean crushing those beneath them. We may feel the way Lincoln did about slavery: "As I would not be a slave, so I will not be a master." Women have been oppressed; so we fear becoming the oppressor. We need new models for being appropriately assertive, taking responsible authority, and learning how to use genuine anger creatively.

The Balance of Power. On another level, however, women fear taking power because we are afraid of power itself. Pragmatically we can work through many of our feelings about power on a conscious level, but unconscious factors may still inhibit us. We are afraid that the dragon within us may get out of control and destroy. It is as though women have been separated into two different types: the Madonna exemplifies purity and innocence—and powerlessness; the Witch exemplifies demonic power. Only the evil woman was allowed to have power. If we have not fully worked through our unconscious destructive potential, we may not be able to integrate power into our lives. Often we polarize the question of power into an either-or or win-lose situation, without considering that it might be possible to change our perspective.

The problem of power can be compared to a seesaw. The person in charge often seems like one who always insists on sitting on the ground at one end of the seesaw; the other person, the lightweight who has no power, is left to dangle her feet impotently. The Me woman often assumes this position because the only alternative she can see is always being in control, and she doesn't want to be the heavyweight all of the time.

But seesaws are remarkable toys for children to learn the balance of power and appropriate use of leverage. A seesaw has several different supports so that people of different weights can shift the center. The heavyweight can take the shorter end; the lightweight the longer end, and they can balance. "Seesaw, Margery Daw: Jack will have a new master" implies that Margery Daw might become Jack's master, but that's up to Margery—she doesn't have to sit on the ground with Jack dangling up in the air. She can balance her power and his so that there can be equality.

We can develop a reciprocal sharing of power, just like we can alternate the support on the seesaw. The Good Witch of the North used power to help, not to destroy.

From Competition and Conflict to Collegiality. The problem of competition and conflict is linked with the problem of power and control. Most of us have a model of authority predicated on the best man winning—or the best woman winning—or the best winning all the time. The image we're used to is the pyramid of power, a dog-eat-dog existence in which men claw their way up the ladders of success, reach plateaus, push their competitors off the cliff, and strain to climb higher and higher. The Peter Principle, the idea that each man rises to his level of incompetence, is an absurdity, a thought disorder of an illogical way of being in the world.

Recently, however, new models have appeared, initially within the upper ranks of big business. Executives finally realized that they were in charge and had power and control, but they had to depend on experts in many fields who worked under them. They had to learn to work *with* their subordinates. New forms of management training stressed that each person in a group needs to be responsible for the task functions of maintaining the group and getting its work done. Instead of a pyramid of power, management is turning increasingly to the process of consultation and cooperation in a spirit of collegiality. Business is recognizing that conflict can lead to creative solutions for apparently unsolvable problems. Individuals are encouraged to speak out in such a way that they don't overidentify with their ideas but feel responsible only to present their perspective honestly in order to get all the facts on the table so that the total group can make decisions based upon all the evidence.

This new way of learning to work in groups is exciting. Back in the late '60s I was doing some free-lance leadership work with a team of trainers for a large group of church leaders. These people were devoted and sincere, but they had one blindspot. They were used to the male hierarchical principle in the church; they expected the man in control to tell them what to do, to have all the ideas, and to be responsible for executing the work. In a training weekend these people were divided into working groups. Each was asked to survey the needs of the total community for the week-end and devise something that would fill that need. At first the people involved were angry with us as trainers. They told us that they wanted to be told what to do and then they would do it. They didn't like struggling with a new model of working together.

By the end of the week-end, each group had presented an entertainment or a service to the total group that was fun, useful, or meaningful. One group prepared a unique worship service for Sunday morning. Several other groups presented entertainments about the process of consultation. They were hilarious—especially the before and after versions of "how-to-work-in-a-group." They had learned that a group of people can learn to function creatively together as a team to provide meaningful answers to group problems. The old problem of hierarchy had changed because the model had changed. Each person had had a chance to feel that what each said was important and mattered to the entire process. This new model is more in keeping with the feminine principle of valuing each family member and nurturing the growth and development of each child equally. It is a model we can use creatively to solve our dilemma about competition, control, and conflict.

THE XYZ'S OF RELATIONSHIPS

After we have worked through the basic ABC's of ego strengths, we are ready to take a look at the important XYZ's of relationships. Women often fear growing and becoming independent because they fear the loss of close dependent relationships they have with loved ones—or they fear they will be unable to find a man if they are "too strong." In their minds, these women link dependency with closeness; to them independence means distance and loneliness.

Actually the reverse is true. Once we reach the I stage and become full-functioning persons, all aspects of interpersonal relationships become better and stronger. The stronger our egos, the better able we are to risk the closeness of a truly intimate relationship. We are able to enjoy both the times we can be together and the times we are apart. We no longer need another to fulfill us. As we feel better about ourselves, we are able to feel better about our loved ones. As we give to ourselves, we are better able to give to others. As we get in touch with our deepest needs and wants, we are able to make them known to others—and able to hear and reciprocate with their needs and wants. As our lives become richer, we have more to share. We are both more interesting ourselves and more interested in others. The more whole we are, the more we are ready for a whole relationship. All aspects important to us as women become richer and fuller. Sex becomes more free and less demanding as we enjoy our bodies fully without earlier inhibitions. We are "turned on" on our own account and able then to help "turn on" others. As we are more able to confide in our loved ones, they begin to feel more comfortable confiding in us. As we are more able to listen to others, they have more incentive to listen to us.

In the I stage we finally reach the true intimacy—emotionally, physically, intellectually—which we longed for unsuccessfully in earlier stages. This in turn can mean the risk of loss and suffering, but it is worth that risk. The more we love, the greater the potential pain; yet to deny love for that reason would be like insisting on living in a desert all our lives instead of enjoying the garden in full bloom in summertime. Life is meant to be lived to its fullest, and the woman who has reached the I state knows that better than anyone else.

STAGE IV

The I/Thou Stage

The Me, Myself, and I stages present a clear-cut developmental sequence of personal identity and skills. Although we may undergo turmoil and tension during the Myself stage, it is nothing like the radical changes that begin the I/Thou stage. There's no definite time when we can expect this stage. It presents a sharp cleavage and discontinuity from the other stages. It's not necessarily inevitable, like menopause if we live long enough. Some people say it begins after the midpoint of life when we begin to face the prospect of death—but some people refuse to face that prospect, while others face it very early, even in their teens.

This is a mysterious stage. Moving into it is not a matter of choice and control. In this period we are forced to recognize the limits of human reason and human capabilities whether we like it or not. We are thrown into it unwillingly, tossed out of the comfortable worlds we have taken for granted. Something totally unexpected happens to us, and we are once again vulnerable as infants because our egos cannot cope. Nothing seems to make sense. We lose all our bearings. It's as though we are journeying through a pitch-dark tunnel, blackness all around, no glimmering of light behind us or before us. We are truly lost. We have to acknowledge our personal limits, which can be a bitter task.

For survival we search for new meaning, new purpose, and new values. We begin listening to the deeper messages within our creative unconscious and get in touch with the transpersonal and the transcendent. Some people would call this a religious stage, but it goes beyond conventional religion. It's a stage when our whole state of mind becomes living by faith.

CHAPTER 8

The Dark Night of the Soul

WHY ME?

Each stage we have examined up to this point presented tasks which seemed to some extent within our capacity to achieve. Difficult as it may be, we can learn how to own our selves instead of disowning parts of ourselves. We can learn to find space for ourselves and stand on our own ground, and we can risk trying new behaviors even when it would be more comfortable to stay within the old patterns.

The movement into the fourth stage is radically different. It is marked at all times by pain—searing, incomprehensible pain—which wipes out all previous conceptions of the world, ourselves, and others. It is precisely the rawness and the unanticipated aspect of the threshold of this stage which convinces me that it is beyond our control. We can neither predict nor control it.

Something happens which zeroes in on our most vulnerable spot in a way that seems unfair, unjust, and totally unreasonable. "Why me, O Lord?" we may scream. There is no way to cope with what has happened; no appeal can be made to any court to change our sentence. What has seemed ours cannot be so any longer. We feel violated, torn, ripped apart, vulnerable, and impotent. The rug has been pulled out from underneath our feet, and we are flat on our backs.

Such events have happened in my life: the death of my father, my eldest daughter's stormy adolescence, the dissolution of my marriage, the terminal illness of one of my dearest loved ones. Every time something within me died—some naivete about life, some presumption that such things could never happen to me. Suddenly *I* was no longer in charge of my universe. Everything I had taken for granted was wiped away. Pain filled my world. Nobody, no thing could help. I was naked, vulnerable—and alone before God. And there was nothing I could find to hope for nor to celebrate. I was flat on my back and no earthly power could have gotten me up again. It seemed right then that not even prayer could help. I felt deserted and abandoned, especially by God. Absolute despair would turn to anger. How could God let this happen to me? Why me?

At such times it seems as though life can no longer be measured in years or months or even days. Only the moment exists in which I don't know how I will be able to keep going, when all I want to do is dig my head in the sand, collapse on my bed, curl up and die. Sleep is the one escape, for it stops the endless circling in my head of, What can I do? What can be done? How can I keep on going? Tears help if they come, but even then there comes a time when one is all cried out and the pain is still there.

I have been with a few others as they were going through dark nights of the soul. Somehow in their grief and agony, they were not quite in the same room with me but locked deep in some inner recess I could not reach. No matter how much I cared and wanted to help, the only thing I could do was be there, be present so they would know I was standing by.

Moments like this are just about impossible to describe, nor would it be appropriate to do so in detail. This is where old friends who know our history are so important. We don't have to speak—because we can't. Yet somehow in making new friends we can point to such times, and, if they've been there too, we don't have to describe what it was like to them either. There is a companionship of survivors in which certain recognition signals are passed without words even though we may have entered the abyss by different doors.

A CONSPIRACY OF SILENCE

Even though we cannot share directly the intimate details of these moments, we do our selves a great disservice to ignore their existence. I really wrestled whether or not I would include this stage in this book. Too much of me has been conditioned by our society; we hide behind masks, never share our deepest feelings, paste a happy smile on our faces, grit our teeth, and keep on going alone. Even though I needed to own my times of absolute despair as part of the wholeness of my life, part of me questioned parading them in public. I suspect writers who plead how much they have suffered; that seems inauthentic and phony. So I am reticent to bring up this aspect of what I've been calling growth and development. How can I write about what can't be spoken about? But how can I be real without doing so?

The one thing that broke into my ambivalence and conflict was remembering what Martin Luther, the Protestant reformer, said so long ago about human suffering. Luther had penetrating insights into the way we live which came out in his sermons to people of his time. One thing he kept repeating—which no one seemed to hear—was that the incomprehensibleness of pain and despair in our lives leads us to recognize who we are before God. Otherwise we construct gods of our own devising (he predated Freud in knowing that) and think we are the source of our glory and accomplishments.

Luther had little patience with the so-called Christian saints of his time, that is, those persons who deliberately sought suffering in order to glory in carrying their cross and following Christ. No, he insisted, life sends us enough pain without our having to create our own. He was cutting into the needless masochism of those artificial imitators of Christ and pointing to a deeper reality. In those authentic moments of unanticipated suffering when finally we reach out to the Lord, we discover the meaning of living by faith. Then our lives are transformed.

We must speak about such moments as an integral part of our

existence. We must own them because they transform what would otherwise be a flat two-dimensional existence. We must own them because in them we are touched by eternity and the transcendent.

NEW DIMENSIONS

In that special little book, *The Prophet,* Kahlil Gibran has one line I wish could be given to each child at birth, perhaps on an engraved bracelet: "Your pain is the breaking of the shell of your understanding." As it is, most of the time we seem to muddle through life in the false illusion that if somehow we could be good enough we might go back to the days of innocence and beauty and light, back to the nostalgic warmth of paradise and Eden in our mothers' arms.

But if we are to be a growing, developing species, our learning will come by means of the suffering we incur when earlier stages of life are swept away. It can be very painful for a baby to be weaned unless he or she is able to trust mother's goodness even when she denies her breast. Toddlers incur endless bumps and hurts as they smash into things while learning to walk. Athletes learn that they can push themselves past a certain level of exhaustion into a stage of getting their "second wind." Mothers giving birth can learn how to go with the process of labor so that they don't tighten up and increase their pain.

Similarly, in recovering from the first shock of what I called the "searing incomprehensible pain" which marks the threshold of stage four, we can begin to reorient ourselves in a new dimension. We can note its various aspects and explore them: (1) the incomprehensibleness, when our previous "shell of understanding" is broken; (2) the involuntary aspect, when that shell has been broken against our will; (3) pain; and (4) the alternatives and choices in this new realm.

SHELLS OF UNDERSTANDING

In the I/Thou stage: the world we have known goes to pieces, and the *I* of the ego and the self we have been working so hard to exercise and develop is threatened. All the dreams, plans, and expectations, all the plain everydayness of life, have been knocked apart. All the bits and pieces of our lives are spread out, and we can't get them back together.

The truth is, the *I* can't get things back together because the rational ego-understanding which has been getting us through has been knocked out. The rules that applied before no longer work. We scramble hard at first to put things back together the way they used to be, but nothing can ever be quite the same. We try hard to deny the change and to patch up what we can with a lot of superstick glue, but it doesn't work very well. Often we begin tip-toeing around life instead of meeting it head-on.

What we have to face, and what we don't want to face, is that we are not masters of our fate. We don't know the rules in the new dimension, but we keep trying to impose the old ones.

We don't want to see that we have been assuming that our own particular illusion of life constituted all of reality, and it can now no longer do that for us. We need to find some other way to understand reality beyond what we have presumed. Sociologist Peter Berger has explained how reality is socially determined and constructed, just as games children play are invented to meet particular life situations. Reality as we know it is a carefully managed balancing of our environment, the tools and techniques which have been invented to manipulate that environment, and the culture, that is, language, arts, and sciences, which provides a framework for living within our givens. Erikson has given examples of the various ways in which each culture structures the care of its infants to meet the identities determined by the physical environment; for instance, the Sioux Indians who had plenty of space to roam were able to allow their children more freedom than the Yurok Indians who were constrained to live carefully confined lives along the rivers in which they caught salmon.

Perhaps it's easier to see what this means on a large scale. When a catastrophe occurs, such as a flood, hurricane, tornado, war, or the massive power failure in the eastern United States back in 1965, people suddenly begin to relate in new ways. Some collapse; others care, share and help strangers. Others react as though they can do anything they want to since all the usual means of maintaining law and order have been swept away; they rip, tear, loot, try to grab what they can, and increase the general destruction.

Stripped of old *I*dentities and normal patterns, we have the opportunity to create out of chaos; for a while we may even rejoice in an uncommon freedom before we have to reassemble and resume the old roles and old scripts. Disaster movies like *Earthquake* and *The Towering Inferno* serve as equivalent rehearsals for each of us to experience vicariously the massive dislocation of normal reality.

In our individual lives there is little we can do to rehearse ahead of time. In movies and books we may empathize with the tragic death of a child and perhaps gain some secondhand experience of what it might be like to go on living after such a personal catastrophe. We may read about or see how a person knocked down and out slowly begins to recover. We may study Transactional Analysis and know all about how we act as Parent, Adult, or Child. But when the chips are down, none of these ego-states can do any more than temporarily tide us over. Intellectually we may understand what has happened to us, but the feeling of impotence and pain paralyzes us.

POWERLESSNESS

In our culture we can take anything, I think, except powerlessness. Strength is somehow equated with the power to *accomplish* anything rather than with the courage to *endure* something. Psychologist Andreas Angyal once said that we would rather be guilty than weak. Powerlessness is that absolute feeling of impotence which reduces us to the status of a child unable to fend for herself. We fight desperately against having to admit that we cannot take care of ourselves.

Once we have reached a position of *I*dentity, of independence and ability, we fight desperately against having to admit that we can't make it on our own. Once we have found our selves, our great need is to assert "I can do it" and to keep on giving rather than having to take or ask for help. We would rather minister unto than be ministered unto; we would rather be the one who is "caring for" than to be "taken care of." The tragedy in nursing homes is that the elderly have no role other than patient and being cared for; they have no sense of being able to contribute.

We have been brainwashed into thinking that it is always better to give than to receive, but we never stop to consider that when we are always in the giving role we force others into the receiving position, into impotence and patienthood. How happy to be the Red Cross Nurse, the great Lady Bountiful, always dispensing gifts and receiving the adoration that role demands! How rare the capacity to facilitate the growth of others into a position of equality and mutuality!

Even women with *I*dentity can fall into the Red Cross Nurse trap. The danger of independence is that it becomes brittle and polarized into not being able to be mutually interdependent, into not being able to be dependent in a healthy fashion upon those who "care" for us. We march along proudly, self-assured and self-confident, having slain all our dragons of Me and Myself. The last thing we want is to feel once again that everything is happening to us.

But somehow life will not let us remain in that puffed-up position. A woman who has undergone many tragedies in her life told me that just as soon as she thinks she has it made, something else comes along and wipes her off her feet. She wasn't being masochistic or enjoying her pain but pointing to the inevitability of remaining forever in the position of narcissistic self-will.

Something within our greater selfhood doesn't want us to exalt ourselves too highly. This position is a psychological state called ego-inflation in which the I, the ego, insists upon being the all-powerful center of our lives. Such inflation must be pricked like a balloon in order for the ego-center to give way and to allow for growth in new dimensions.

The sense of powerlessness leads us, if we will allow it, to recognize a Power and a Wisdom beyond our own. In this process our ego relinquishes its position in the center of our psyche and allows the true sense of Self, or our soul, to take its proper place. The changeover from ego to soul is as different a state of being as AM and FM on the radio. My ego-style of living is full of static like AM; my soul is tuned in differently and has the potential for stereophonic sound in which this life becomes related to a Greater Life just as time is related to eternity.

PAIN

Our reactions to pain and suffering are as unique as each one of us; some may withdraw from life, refusing future involvements, saying "once burned, twice shy"; others may deny their loss and be unable to cry; still others block off feeling any pain by turning to narcotizing activities and drugs; some cling to pain, wet-nursing it, using it as an alibi to regress into childlike dependence; a few learn to live with suffering as a part of their particular reality which cannot be transmuted. Some women react stoically to pain; others fall apart. Some refuse to talk; others are garrulous in endlessly recounting their personal tragedies to whomever will listen.

Pain comes in a number of ways: a small child cries when a new balloon pops; a young girl is devastated when she doesn't make the cheerleading team; a woman grieves over the loss of a stillborn child. In our losses, failures, broken dreams, and broken hearts, we undergo an invisible wounding of our spirit. Since we are creatures born and reared in love, the loss of a loved one causes a deep breach within us which takes time to heal. Since we are creatures of dreams, when they are disappointed, we grieve. Unless we are hermits, we cannot avoid attachments or involvements. Consequently, our very selfhood is wounded when such attachments are broken.

With any real loss, there is need for a genuine period of mourning which we must work through completely so that we can let go afterward and go on living. All too often, we tend to shorten the grief period. There is a way going down deeply into the pain, like the deep cleansing of a flesh wound, so that we can heal again instead of getting an infected wound which lingers endlessly. By going down into the pain, I do not mean a morbid or masochistic fascination with grief as an entity in itself, but a facing of the loss, honoring it, and then letting it go. I used to hate the phrase "Let go and let God," but I have learned that until I really accept the reality of my loss as fact and let it go, I prolong my agony.

Somehow we need to sort out the suffering we have, in a manner similar to the attitudes toward change in the serenity prayer: "Lord, grant me the courage to change what can be changed; the serenity to accept what cannot be changed; and the wisdom to know the difference." Somehow we need to be able to pray, "Lord, grant me the strength to endure the suffering I cannot change; the wisdom to learn from the suffering into which my errors have led me; and the serenity to deal with whatever suffering I am going through." ·

Such a prayer would help us begin to reevaluate our lives, to sort out our priorities, and to learn even from situations which brought us the greatest pain. It seems that some tests and sufferings keep coming back until we make an inner change in our attitudes and begin to examine our alternatives in life.

CHAPTER 9

Growing Edges

Pain . . . powerlessness . . . meaninglessness. In the midst of the soul-wrenching experiences which lead into the dark night of the soul, these three feelings may seem to be the only dimensions of our existence. It is as though we are in a dark tunnel. We have lost all the hope and trust which have gotten us through life this far. The old dreams have been wiped away, the old relationships have been shattered, and it seems that we are truly alone.

All through this book I have talked about discerning alternatives and making choices. But what possible alternatives can we see, what possible choices can we make, when everything seems to be wiped away?

I feel like a toddler in this new sphere of existence. I look at my life and know that I have been given very much. My darkest moments seem slight compared to those of other women. Elizabeth was a linguist. Her first husband and their only child, a month-old son, were killed in a meaningless air raid in Austria just after the Germans surrendered. She somehow managed somehow to stay alive, wending her way on foot across war-desolated Europe to a sanctuary in southern France where old friends lived. Catherine was a beautiful pianist. Her potential concert career was wiped out completely after her left hand was crushed in a car accident. Sylvia's husband underwent a schizophrenic break and died in a sanitarium only weeks after the birth of their only daughter. Helen's lovely adolescent daughter committed suicide. Theresa died a long, lingering death from cancer of the liver. Vivian is still surviving with chronic leukemia. Margaret's husband died from chronic alcoholism one year after her father died of cancer.

These women, who came from a variety of religious backgrounds, all managed somehow to go on living in a new way. Despite everything that happened, they reordered their lives and their priorities. Their view of reality is entirely different from that of other women I know who have been safely protected and have not borne such tests. These women are real. They are whole persons, despite—or because of—the horrendous scars they bear on their souls. They serve as witnesses that it is possible to go through the valley of the shadow of death and find new meaning in life.

The courage they have wipes out any neurotic fear of change or risk. It is as though once your system has undergone sufficient shock, everything else shifts around. In a way, it's similar to what has been called culture shock. Once I asked a man from Europe what sort of culture shock he had when he came to the United States immediately after World War II. He smiled at my naivete and then explained that one can undergo radical culture shock only once, as he had during the war. After that something shifted inside in terms of the way he viewed life. Another person who had faced death many times, from tuberculosis of the bone to polio, when told he had leukemia, said, "What else is new?"

There is a style of living, a way of life, on the other side of death and nothingness which transcends the states of Me, Myself, and I. Only rarely do we find it portrayed in mass media presentations. Soap operas often deal with life-shattering situations, such as the tragic death of a young doctor ("The Doctors"), a husband ("The Young and the Restless'), and the potentially terminal illness of a young husband ("Search for Tomorrow"). In such shows, we see, not only the appalling shock of the unexpected, ripping into the lives of favorite characters, but also how they face and deal with their incredible losses. The pain and suffering they feel is generally depicted in silence because words cannot carry the depth of the emotion.

BOUNDARIES

In these moments, we realize first that we have reached the boundary lines of our personhood. You may hear someone say at such times (as if it might help) that God has said a person will not be tested beyond his or her capacity. That sounds to me as if God were more a devil, carefully calculating just how much pain and suffering we might be able to take on our personal Richter scale, pushing a test button to see if the figures were right, and upping the intensity of pain until we reach our limits. I can't believe in that sort of God.

I do believe that sometimes we smash ourselves against a wall of understanding because we have violated a spiritual law of existence. Perhaps we idolized some aspect of ourselves or some relationship. At other times, the givens of life and death, make our boundary experiences inevitable. The test is not suffering per se but whether we will be able to let go our precious ego boundaries and reach out for that Hand in which is our soul. Once we recognize our limits, we can explore the deeper aspects of ourselves. Reaching out and turning inward are the two major tasks of this life-stage.

REACHING OUT

When we reach our personal limits of endurance, it is normal to want to give up. There are several ways we can do this. We can literally give up and die. Some people cannot imagine living without the persons, things, and circumstances that made up the worlds they took for granted. They commit suicide. Others may attempt to do so but leave enough lee-way to ask for help. They turn themselves over to whoever might rescue them.

Still others give up much more slowly. They manage to go on living but in a self-destructive way. They turn to drink or to drugs or to other violent means of acting out their despair. They ask more subtlely to be put away where life won't hurt so much.

Others are even more subtle. Nothing much matters to them any more. They live out their days without hope in a world of bitter grayness. They continue living within the tunnel, with lifeless eyes and ears, apathetic, just waiting for someone else to blow the whistle on them.

Then there are those with a devil-may-care attitude who proceed through the tunnel. They pretend that if they don't let anything happen to them or hurt them too much they will scrape along. Nothing touches them, nor do they reach out to touch anyone. One woman told me that she'd given up making new friends because it hurt too much when they died or moved away.

People who give up in these four ways keep on going, holding on to the illusion that there is only one world and only one way to live in it. But there is another way to give up. It is turning and asking help from the ultimate source of all help—in prayer.

But praying isn't always easy, especially for those who have given up on God anyway. The strange thing, however, is that we can point to examples of prayers uttered in just such situations. The Book of Psalms, for instance, in the Old Testament of the Bible, is filled with words of bitterness and despair against God for what has happened to the psalmist:

I am weary with my moaning;
    every night I flood my bed with tears;
    I drench my couch with my weeping.
My eye wastes away because of grief,
    it grows weak because of all my foes (Ps. 6:6–7, RSV).

How long, O Lord? Wilt thou forget me for ever?
    How long wilt thou hide thy face from me?
How long must I bear pain in my soul,
    and have sorrow in my heart all the day?
How long shall my enemy be exalted over me? (Ps. 13:1–2, RSV).

And in Psalm 22, which contains the lines Christ spoke from the cross, we hear a person in absolute despair:

> My God, my God, why hast thou forsaken me?
>   Why art thou so far from helping me, from the
>   words of my groaning?
> O my God, I cry by day, but thou dost not answer;
>   and by night, but find no rest. . . .
> I am poured out like water,
>   and all my bones are out of joint;
> my heart is like wax,
>   it is melted within my breast;
> my strength is dried up like a potsherd,
>   and my tongue cleaves to my jaws;
>   thou dost lay me in the dust of death (Ps. 22:1–2, 14–15, RSV).

Such despair is not unusual. In fact, it can mark the transition point between merely living an ordinary life and living a life filled with faith. When we finally cry out to God—in anger, desperation, or hopelessness—we confess our finitude and ask for help. Then comes a response which cannot be recorded scientifically but is preserved in many religious writings. Near the end of each penitential psalm, there is a pause and a turning point.

> . . . for the Lord has heard the sound of my weeping,
> . . . has heard my supplication;
> . . . accepts my prayer (Ps. 6:8–9, RSV).

> But I have trusted in thy steadfast love;
>   my heart shall rejoice in thy salvation.
> I will sing to the Lord,
>   because he has dealt bountifully with me (Ps. 13:5–6, RSV).

> You who fear the Lord, praise him!
>   all you sons of Jacob, glorify him,
>   and stand in awe of him, all you sons of Israel!
> For he has not despised or abhorred
>   the affliction of the afflicted;
> and he has not hid his face from him,
>   but has heard, when he cried to him (Ps. 22:23–24, RSV).

The Old Testament Book of Job presents the prototype of a good man who cried out to God, screaming against the injustice of his suffering. After God replied to him with a magnificent hymn to human finitude, Job confessed his ignorance before the Lord and affirmed his new faith. In the Garden of Gethsemane, despite his anguish, Christ affirmed "Not my will, but thine be done"; and then he was able to conclude his hours of suffering on the cross with "Into thy hands I commend my spirit." Baha'u'llah, the prophet-founder of the Baha'i Faith, was imprisoned and exiled for forty years. In the Fire Tablet he cried out with despair to God, "Thou has forsaken Me in a strange land; where are the emblems of Thy faithfulness, O Trust of all the worlds!" And, after a response from God, he responded in faith, "Surely I have heard Thy call, O All-Glorious Beloved; . . . Baha hath risen up in faithfulness at the place of sacrifice, looking toward Thy pleasure, O Desire of the worlds."[2]

It seems that once we can let go efforts to save ourselves, a spiritual force comes to sustain us. Once we allow ourselves to die to the old pattern of life, we can be reborn with a new respect for the wonder of life. We become like little children. We have a new way of being in the world. Even the simplest things become precious.

Whether or not we are able to take such a leap of faith and receive a spiritual sense of renewal, there are still tasks to be worked through during this state as we tune into the inner voice of our psyche.

INNER TASKS

The shock of painful experiences serves for many women as the beginning of a period of transition, a kind of death and rebirth from one way of being in the world to another. The dark tunnel of unknowing serves as a threshold into a new world that can only be reached by the pain of giving up previous presumptions. The period of mourning the old way and the lost world is real and difficult.

The major shift during this period is that our ego, our I self, is no longer the center of our selfhood. We acquire a new center, a new way of being in the world in which we can get some "role-distance" from everything that happens. The old games and the old scripts lose the power they may have had over us. We become free from the trap of ego-tism and are able to see it as a vital, necessary part of our development which we have grown beyond. With this new shift, at long last we have the potential to be free-floating, to fly and soar as the birds. The cage of the ego is the most seductive of all cages, and working free of it can be as complicated as developing it to start with. Our goal is to reach inside toward our creative depths.

As we turn inside, we gradually have to deal with the deeper layers of selfhood left unlabelled in the scribble drawing we did back in chapter seven. Jungian psychologists have studied this period of development and given it the name of *individuation,* a time for developing that sense of wholeness and completeness which is often represented by a circular figure known as a *mandala.* Dreams have been called the royal road to the unconscious, and by working with our dreams over an extended period we can get in touch with powerful unconscious forces which influence us in many ways. Working with dreams without a therapist is difficult, but it can be done alone, or at least begun that way. The main task is to keep a regular daily journal of every dream you can remember. Each morning, make a few careful notes of what happened in your dreams the night before, as well as how you felt about those dreams and any associations you have with them. Do they seem related to something specific in your life or something you anticipate in the future? Dreams are ambiguous and have many layers of meaning. Some may appear to be just a nightly form of entertainment that serves to keep us asleep. Other dreams serve as wish-fulfillment or compensation for what is not happening in our waking life. But other dreams present the foretelling and unfolding of our selfhood in new, unanticipated ways.

One of the most helpful ways to keep track of your dreams is to follow particular groups of images which may repeat themselves. Following various images of female figures may give us clues about the unexplored aspects of our feminine nature. Images of men are more apt to be related to our undeveloped masculine side. There is no one rule of thumb, however. Dream images can carry many different levels of meaning simultaneously. One key image which does seem to relate to a newfound sense of the deeper self as whole and complete is the image of a new baby. The important thing is to follow your own images and allow your unconscious to speak to you.

In doing so you may find one particular image which is really meaningful. I found one key image for me in a dream I worked through with one of my therapists. In the dream was a victim— myself, a man who stole my purse, and a beautiful white bird that flew after the man, rescued my purse, and brought it back to me. I began working with the dream as if I were only the victim, but my therapist led me to recognize that I was also the bird. He had me imagine in detail what it would be like to fly as that bird did. As I described how that bird was free to soar and climb, coast and glide, stretching its wings to use all its strength, I began getting in touch with a side of me I had not realized. The image of that bird is still special for me. It's an image somewhere near the heart of who I am when I'm really tuned in to myself. It's me when I am living out of my creative center. It's the time when my own spirit is able to climb, and soar, and be free.

Owning that bird as an aspect of myself is just one step in the process of learning to own all the aspects of myself I encounter in my dreams. The bird was a positive aspect which I enjoyed recognizing, but other aspects have been more difficult to accept. The unknown aspects, which we have rejected and disowned and consciously don't want, often pop up in dreams. Jung grouped all these aspects into the concept of the *Shadow*. Often that which we cannot tolerate in ourselves becomes precisely what we can least tolerate in other people. As long as we haven't come to terms with these aspects, we project them onto other people who then serve as targets for the projections of our unintegrated parts. Others become the victims of our inner prejudices against ourselves.

In one respect, however, this Shadow side for women can pull a switch on us. Often we have buried in our Shadow many of our undeveloped positive aspects. Consciously we are aware of our negative points; unconsciously we have repressed the possibility of actually being able to achieve our goals. The fear many women have of success is linked to their unknown Shadow.

The great thing about coming to terms with our Shadow is that the more we accept all parts of ourselves, the more real we can become with other people. As we work through assimilating the Shadow, that outer shell (labeled 4B in the scribble) begins to dissolve. Jung termed this outer shell the *Persona*. It's like the masks the early Greek actors wore to represent the role they were playing on stage. Most of us tend to have glittering, shiny-mirror Personas so that we will reflect the good things we think other people want to see. Peculiarly enough many women bury their best half within their Shadows so they can project it on to someone upon whom they're dependent. Then they cloak themselves in drab Personas (all unconsciously). But many such seemingly weak little pussycats turn out to have roaring tigers lurking inside! Dealing with the Persona is difficult because we have to come to terms with the Shadow.

Another major part of the unconscious we have to come to terms with is our undeveloped masculine side. Jung called this aspect within women the *Animus,* and he termed the feminine side of men the *Anima.* In the discussion about the spell of romantic love, I mentioned that many couples are linked together originally because each carries for the other the undeveloped side of the opposite sex. Woman plays out the role of man's undeveloped feminine aspects and serves as his Anima; men often play out our undeveloped masculine aspects as the Animus. Burt Reynolds, Paul Newman, and Robert Redford all serve as collective representations of the Animus for millions of women, and Marilyn Monroe is the classic example of at least one form of the Anima.

But, like everything else in the unconscious, the Animus shifts and changes over the years. Animus figures vary from woman to woman and within a woman from one stage of her life to others. During the process of individuation we learn to recognize and deal with our inner mysterious Animus. The goal is a sort of inner marriage or union, which Jung believed was the necessary prerequisite for becoming linked with our creative depths and the center of our psyche, which he termed officially the *Self*. The Animus serves as an inner bridge for women, just as the Anima does for men. Just as men must connect with their inner soul figure of the Anima in order to become creative, so women must connect with the Animus. Women who fail to do this remain blocked in several ways. Some play the role of Anima, much as the sex symbol Marilyn Monroe seemed to represent. Others play out a brisk sort of mannish role, as if their Animus was on the outside as a Persona instead of on the inside. As long as we have not integrated the Animus, we tend to look for all the masculine aspects of ourselves outside. We search endlessly for an ideal male to play out that role for us.

Working through these unconscious aspects leads eventually to that sense of true integrity and wholeness as persons pointed to by many religions. The New Testament records Jesus saying "Be ye perfect." The Greek word translated "perfect" is *teleos* and means "complete" or "whole." It is the same word Jesus used on the cross when he said, "It is finished," meaning he had completely fulfilled his task. Our lives need to have that sense of being whole and complete, good points with the bad, instead of the former misconception that to be perfect meant being 99 44/100 percent pure—like Ivory Soap.

LOOKING AHEAD

Regardless of whether you use the traditional imagery of religious faith or the more contemporaneous insights of depth psychology, or both, as I do, the net effect is the same. Moving into the fourth stage results from and produces a tremendous shift in our lives. The loss of all previous centers results in a complete reordering of our lives and requires a new orientation period. Many of our previous values reverse as we become more sensitive to the transcendent mystery which surrounds us.

In each previous stage there has been a natural tension over what will be the center of our lives. During the Me stage we are content to center upon someone else. During the Myself stage we gradually take new responsibility for our lives as part of the natural, normal development of the ego. During the I stage we find our center of awareness and action, and we are able to bear the necessary separation which is part of being a unique individual.

During the fourth stage something new replaces everything that has occupied the center of our lives. The great Jewish philosopher-theologian Martin Buber referred to the possibility of this new relationship as the I/Thou mode of life. This way of being in the world means that I relate to everything in my life both out of my own wholeness and in response to the wholeness of everyone and everything else. It is as though everything and everyone is contained within the primary relationship of love. However, we only realize this I/Thou relationship in fleeting moments. Most of the time we continue to be caught in the more impersonal, objective type of relationship which Buber termed the I/it.

One way of describing the I/Thou way of being in the world in contrast to the I/it is that most of the time we live in a world of various shades of gray, like the pictures on a black-and-white television set. But occasionally the whole world is transformed by technicolor. In such peak moments we realize that life possesses a transcendent beauty beyond our understanding. Knowing this means that we can begin to change the way we respond to the black-and-whiteness. We can consciously begin to strive to increase the potential of technicolor for everyone.

But, you may ask, aren't we able to have religious faith in the previous stages of consciousness? If ultimately we all are dependent before God, what's the difference between the first and the fourth stage?

The answer to these questions is complex. Søren Kierkegaard, the Danish theologian, spent the major portion of his career endeavoring to lay out the stages along life's way in religious development. Briefly, it seems as though we move in a spiral. In the Me stage we have a simple, child-like unquestioned faith. Our pattern of religious tradition is generally inherited from our parents, as the first-born described by William James in *Varieties of Religious Experience.* During the

Myself stage, we grow in consciousness and lose our innocence. We set up neurotic religious patterns to handle guilt and shame. We think our salvation is up to our own good works. We deny awareness of sin, splitting ourselves individually. We alternate between being a good, pious person on Sunday or Sabbath and a back-slider during the week. In the I stage, quite often religious faith is dismissed along with Santa Claus and the Easter Bunny. We become mistresses of our own fate: God is dead, and religious ritual often hollow and meaningless.

The I/Thou stage brings us to our knees again. Our faith may appear simple as a child's, but it has been tempered by fire. We are forced into the valley of search and must seek out new answers to ultimate questions. Kierkegaard's knight of faith appeared like every other man—but he had made the "leap of faith" that made all the difference between first-hand and second-hand religious conviction.

In the I/Thou stage we see the ordinary world with new eyes. We realize its finitude and limitations. We begin working for positive change. The personal becomes more important, and every relationship becomes charged with new potential. I don't suppose we will realize what this potential could be, but I do believe that knowing it exists can endow us with new meaning, purpose, and value.

CONCLUSION

The Eternal Feminine

A SPECIAL DAY

Have you ever had a special day in your life? A quiet day you'd like to keep in a drawer and take out occasionally to hold and treasure in the years to come? A day when the pieces of your life seemed to come together for awhile and you got in touch with a rare serenity? A day when everything seemed to be whole despite the fragmentation and tensions around you?

I had a day like that during the summer of 1976 when I was working on this book. It was filled with surprises and unanticipated moments—some of which I helped to make happen, and others which seemed to occur like gifts from persons around me. This day was filled with growing edges and with new doors opening up after several months of my dragging along as I tried to get things back together personally after a long hard winter of discontent and a spring filled with hard work.

It was a day in which all the polarities in my life stood out clearly. I was having to balance tensions which crisscrossed in three directions: between family and work, between old and new relationships, between reaching out professionally while I was still in training myself. I was managing to cope, but I felt stretched in all directions and certainly at the limit of my capacity.

On the one hand I was working hard to finish this book by its contract deadline, trying to find extra hours of quietness to think and work. On the other hand, I wanted to savor the specialness of the preparations for my second daughter's wedding. We had searched through several stores without finding the dress she wanted, and then found it waiting for her almost specially. We'd shared the fun of a kitchen shower attended by mothers and daughters we knew. It was fun to see the gadgets friends couldn't live without—some of which I'd never seen. It was even more fun that there weren't any duplicates!

At the same time I was feeling poignantly the tension between trying to hang on to the old pattern of life I had known in a previous relationship and yet beginning to discern the possibilities for new patterns. I was grieving over the loss of an old love, working through accepting the finality of all that could not be realized between us. I knew I did not want to stay closeted with old memories, that I was starting to be aware of other friendships just beginning.

And then, I could not help feeling the tension between working with other women in their growth stages, while I was continuing therapy and supervision in order to work through my own growth areas. I could feel personally the line of growth which stretches between women in various stages. I know we move toward a distant goal; yet, somehow, I still keep thinking that maybe someday I might have a sense of closure instead of always living on the growing edge.

All these things were going through my mind as I got ready for a day in New York City. I was due in town for three appointments which I had scheduled too close together: 9:30 A.M., uptown near Columbus Circle for supervision in marriage counseling; 11 A.M., farther uptown and across Central Park for personal therapy; 1 P.M., downtown Fifth Avenue to consult on a public relations program for the counseling center in New Jersey where I worked.

Nothing went right in the beginning. I just missed the 8:12 train which would have gotten me into town in plenty of time; the modern 8:18 which I really liked better never showed up; and the 8:26 which I finally took was old and decrepit—and got me into town so late that I had to take a taxi. My supervisor was kind enough to let our session run past its normal time, but that meant I had to take another taxi to make the next appointment.

I settled back in the cab to eat my midmorning yogurt, and suddenly I was in touch with the marvel of the day—clear, crisp and sunny, more like spring than summer. I began reflecting that each day needs to be good in itself, that I couldn't look back too much or forward too much because the "now" is all we ever have.

Then I began to flow with the tempo of the day. I noticed the cab driver drinking his can of soda-pop as he relaxed at the stoplights on Central Park West. He had long hair and was wearing a white garment, rather Far Eastern, with a white neckpiece. I was curious about what sort of meaning that might have; so I got up enough courage to ask him. He was a young American from near Chicago, a member of a Buddhist yoga group. He showed me the special prayer beads he'd been holding in his left hand while driving. No wonder he'd been driving so serenely uptown and through the park! He was interested in knowing about me as well and my membership in the Baha'i Faith. He was acquainted with the writings of Baha'u'llah, especially *The Seven Valleys*,[3] and compared them with the spiritual journey in which Buddhists believe. I talked with him for nearly ten minutes about kundalini yoga, the unity of prophetic writings, and the relation between psychology and religion. I was particularly interested in what he said about opening up the fourth chakra of the heart and love, which he believes is what all the prophets were teaching at different times in world history.

After that, the day took on an even more special hue. At noon I joined a friend in the little park at Fifth Avenue and Twenty-third Street. There was really no way she and I could concentrate on checking pageproofs for the printing she'd designed. We were overwhelmed by the diversity of the people around us—children climbing a valiant little tree; lovers sitting in the crannied nook of a statue: a handsome woman with a pure Earth Mother physique; hawkers for a multitude of addictions from popsicles to soda pop, beer, and pot. The richness of the city's population and the merging of all sorts of backgrounds and costumes was like a rich holiday pudding. I marveled at the genius of New York where so many cultures meet and mingle, at that moment most peacefully and pleasantly.

Later on my way home I stopped in a small shop selling articles

from the Far East: wood carvings of Buddhas, both sitting and danc-
ing; glazed china statuettes of other figures. A friend who was living
in Macau near Hong Kong had sent me a prayer sheet written in
Chinese. It was a sort of special announcement given only to the
worshippers, not to the tourist trade, at a special six-hundred-year-old
temple dedicated to the Buddhist goddess Kuan Yin. The temple
stood on the spot where the first Sino-American pact was signed in
1844. Seeing the store had made me wonder if I could find out more
about the goddess and perhaps buy a small statue to add to my
mini-museum of religious objects.

The people in the store, one woman from Shanghai and two men,
were delighted and fascinated with the prayer sheet. They exclaimed
over it in Chinese. The owner explained what all the little circles down
each side of the paper meant; they were to be crossed off one at a time
as the worshipper read the writings from the "Bible" printed under
the picture of the goddess. He was happy to answer my questions and
promised to try to buy me a little book about Kuan-Lin. As he was
wrapping the small white-robed statue he had found for me, he told
about her history as he knew it. He said she had been the third
daughter of a king, that she had refused to marry, which meant that
the king had become very angry and cut off her head, and that she
watches over everyone and is more special to the Chinese and Japa-
nese than the Virgin Mary is to Roman Catholics.

As I walked toward the train, I marveled over what the old Chinese
man had told me. It was the story of the type of goddess who was
"one-in-herself." I had been searching for an image which might
represent an ultimate goal in our growth and development as women,
and "she" had come to meet me.

THE IRREPRESSIBLE VIRGIN: THE GODDESS WHO IS "ONE-IN-HERSELF"

During the past one hundred years anthropologists and art collec-
tors have traveled around the world, studying the wide variety of

countries and cultures and collecting artifacts and pictures of different forms of religious worship. More recently, within the past thirty years, Jungian psychologists have studied the similarities between the various forms of goddesses and have found common themes between different periods. The more research that is done, the more evident it becomes that the earliest forms of religion were not devoted to a single male deity but to a variety of female goddesses during an early preverbal, matriarchal period. We are not surprised to see the tremendous power these feminine figures had during this period; it parallels the power of male gods during the patriarchal period. What is interesting is the new perspective these studies give us into the concept of virginity in those times.

In addition to the various Earth Mother goddesses, there were also moon goddesses who were the most powerful figures and denoted a spiritual aspect of transformation. They possessed the unique attibute of virginity, which did not have anything to do with physiological reality but was an inherent psychological quality and a subjective attitude retained in some unexplained fashion regardless of how much sexual experience she had, how old she became, or how many children she had born. As Esther Harding explains in *Woman's Mysteries,* the moon goddess was not dependent upon any male figure, either father, husband, or son. She was entirely "one-in-herself," possessed by no one at all.

The sole eternal creative force in the universe was considered female in those early cultures. Paternity, in fact, had not yet been discovered. The power of the goddesses and their daughters was absolute in every area, from the heavens to the earth, from plants and animals to their own mysterious power to create something other than themselves, that is, their sons. The incestuous tie between the mother goddesses and their sons was complete. The son was not merely son but also lover and the sacrifice which would perpetuate the eternal life-giving power of the mother.

Later on, in patriarchal cultures, goddesses became dim counterparts to gods who attained power and prestige. They became the ideal of the married woman, clinging, dependent, and totally domesticated, polarized into the typical split between masculine and feminine which we have known up to the present. They lost the capacity for separate existence and were linked in tandem with the gods. Only a few angry goddesses remained, and they played devious tricks on the male gods in order to achieve their ends. Patriarchy emasculated the feminine, boxed in her powers against herself, and forced her to become a mere possession, with young women passing like chattel from father to husband. Women were allowed to develop only those attributes which insured that they would not threaten the male establishment. What had been the complete feminine in the moon goddess became split into the safe virgin on one side and the demonic witch on the other.

Such powerful restrictions suggest, of course, that there was good reason for this constraint. Just as individual men today can become utterly enthralled by women who carry their undeveloped feminine side (or anima), in the earliest days of humanity whole cultures were enthralled by goddesses. Men worshipped at their feet in absolute servitude and, in moments of complete ecstasy, voluntarily castrated themselves and adorned the statues of goddesses with necklaces of their testicles. Matriarchy was not without its perils for the male-in-thrall to the female, anymore than patriarchy has been for women in bondage to the male.

THE REAL WOMAN TODAY

The solution is neither a returning to matriarchy nor allowing patriarchy to remain in control. I realized that one night in a growth group made up of eight women. Each was struggling with problems relating to a demonic witchlike woman in her life, either a mother-in-law, a mother, or her own unrecognized Oedipal tie to her son. I've often seen the result when men have become subservient to women. Frustrated women are having to be both mother and father to their children because of a husband who is absent, either emotionally or physically. They wish for a man who would be a full partner, one who could share reciprocally and intimately in all aspects of family life.

Often these women have just begun to find themselves as individuals, and they desperately wish their husbands could also.

We need to recognize that there is a potential unfolding of the feminine within each woman's life. The Eternal Feminine is more than just the stage of the life-giving Earth Mother who, as a vessel, nurtures and contains the physical and emotional development of children. The Feminine is also meant to reach a spiritual and emotional level so that she can draw out of the creative depths of her unconscious and serve as a vital source of transformation in the world as a whole. She needs to realize her potential for being "one-in-herself" just as she recognizes the male as potentially "one-in-himself."

Yet how can we conceptualize this Eternal Feminine in everyday life? It's fine to talk about virgin goddesses who are one-in-themselves, but it's another thing to see what that would mean in our lives. One step we can take would be to move beyond all the angry talk which has come from feminists and femininity experts, in the women's movement and point toward a category that would transcend both. We need to integrate these aspects into our lives so that a real woman would be in fact a woman who is a whole person as a member of the female sex.

Each girl-child who is born has in her genes the potential of becoming a whole person. She has a double responsibility to develop as a person, not only to herself, but to the whole human race. First, she has the responsibility to establish her identity as a person and to develop her skills and talents. Then, if she chooses to become a mother, she has the additional responsibility of being the sort of mother who will enable her children to grow and develop as whole persons. I don't believe that a woman who has become polarized into the one aspect of being a "total woman" can raise whole children any more than can other women who have been polarized into competing as aggressively as males in the business and professional world. Such polarization creates all sorts of Shadow games; each side condemns the other for what they cannot tolerate within themselves.

What would be the characteristics of such an integrated woman?

First, it wouldn't make any difference where she lived or worked; it wouldn't make any difference whether she was a full-time homemaker, a business person, a student, or retired. Age and position wouldn't make any difference. What I'm talking about is a style of life, that quality of being "one-in-herself."

Second, she would be "centered." I don't mean she would be "self-centered"; that implies a narcissistic form of self-love which excludes others. Nor would she be centered on anyone else. Rather her center would be on a power beyond herself to which she would acknowledge ultimate dependence. It wouldn't make any difference whether or not she actively affirmed some particular religious creed or belonged to an established religious organization per se, but she would be in search of some deeper meaning to life beyond herself. This affirmation of power coming from beyond would give her the capacity to truly love herself and others equally, to bear the tensions of growth and change in the world, and to bear the polarities within herself which are part of being a whole person. This sense of wholeness would mean she would have the potential for realizing the I/Thou dimension in her relationships.

Third, by being centered, she would be able to be both dependent and dependable, according to the situation. She would be able to be both active and passive; able to live in the here-and-now, without sacrificing either the future or the past to her growing and becoming in the present. She would be able to make responsible choices for the future while affirming past values and conserving the necessary ones.

Fourth, most of all, she would be able to live on the boundaries of existence. This is what it means to live by faith. She would be able to feel the pain, regret, and sorrow that come with recognizing limits and finitude. She wouldn't expect herself to be superwoman, just real, acknowledging both her failures and her successes. Because she would be real, she would also be able to accept the limits and potentialities of other persons. She wouldn't need to project onto them her good or bad parts. She would see others as potentially whole, real persons in themselves.

As a real woman in the home, she would be able to get beyond the games women play as part of the spells they've been caught in or the patterns chosen by the "total" or "fascinating" women. Both her husband and her children would have a chance to realize their wholeness.

Or if she were working as a real woman out in the "world," she would be able to assert herself appropriately. She would be able to fight for the feminine values of personhood which have been suppressed in the past. She wouldn't have to model herself on the successful business "man" to make it, but she would continue to include her feminine values in whatever she did. She would find ways to make caring and concern for others part of the business world as well as in her personal life at home.

THE ROAD AHEAD

When we look back on the first phase of the women's movement, we see that we've just begun to uncover the bare bones of the social structures within Western culture. We've just begun to sort out the various perspectives people have had from where they have been located in that structure. We have seen the women excluded from male structures fight both for inclusion and for benefits from that system. In order to do so they have often sacrificed the "feminine" values our process of child rearing has refused little boys. Conversely, the totally, fascinating women have been hard at work to maintain their roles within the female ghettoes of powerlessness, exacting a heavy toll in manipulation and subversion on the home front.

Two basic structures of meaning have operated in a complementary way. Each has depended on the other to maintain the balance of power within the social system as a whole. The basically white male hierarchy has had most of the money, power, and control to maintain that perspective. Little boys have been raised in ways which have programmed their consciousness to accept the assigned male roles within this establishment. Conversely, little girls and minority persons of both sexes have been programmed to fit the necessary complementary back-up structures. This system has had a powerful momentum which continues to sustain itself.

During the next phase of the women's movement as more women become fully integrated, whole, and real, we will have to face two serious needs. First, the forms of mothering which have perpetuated the old system will have to be changed—and should begin changing as mothers of small children encourage both boys and girls to experience many options for personal growth. We will need more women at home who are capable of doing a real job of mothering "whole-earth" type children so that all children will have the capacity to survive in our increasingly psychotic world. We need more and better mothering today, and we need new community support structures. Today's character disorders, delinquents, and suicides are the products of a culture which has not seen fit to build such structures and has left young mothers to cope alone in the desperate vacuum of the nuclear family. Persons engaged in mothering need to feel the total support of the community behind their essential role.

Second, we need to invent new structures, working with both men and women to invent organizations and social modalities which are different from the matriarchal and patriarchal patterns of the past. There are countless unmet needs in this country and even more in the rest of the world. Third World women are challenging us most directly in this area. But what about the illiterate women in this country? What about the increasing rate of illiteracy in women around the world? What about children of migrant laborers? Occasionally boycotting lettuce in suburbia will not give them a sense of dignity and self-respect. That's a person-to-person job sorely neglected. What about the pockets of despair in the wealthiest areas? What about the acres of decay on one-way streets to oblivion in Watts, California?

We won't know what the world of the future will be until we begin to be creative, with both men and women turning their mutual energies toward the unresolved personal issues which confront us. The integrated, whole woman working with a man similarly integrated and whole will begin to find new ways for the suppressed, repressed "feminine" values of personhood to become part of a new social reality. We don't need to bomb or tear up old institutions that aren't working. All we need do is turn off their switches and refuse to be co-opted into old power structures.

Change is in the wind, and we will see groups begin to change just as we see individuals. Change can open the doors to new dialogue between people, and out of new dialogue we can work together in new ways. We can establish new priorities to match our value systems. We can maintain a new ethical awareness which we need in order to replace that old patriarchal morality of the stern (but fake) superego which went down the drain at Watergate.

The inner changes which women work through on their own in small ways one day at a time will gradually be matched by the shift in outer realities. Whole integrated women joining with whole integrated men will make the difference.

For Further Reading

BOOKS ABOUT THE WOMEN'S MOVEMENT AND THE HISTORY AND
EVOLUTION OF CONSCIOUSNESS.

Berger, Peter L., and Luckmann, Thomas. *The Social Construction of Reality.*
Garden City: Doubleday, 1966.

Boulding, Kenneth E. *The Image.* Ann Arbor Paperbacks. The University of
Michigan Press, 1963.

Buck, Pearl S. *The Complete Woman.* Edited by C. Merton Babcock. Kansas
City, Missouri: Hallmark Cards, 1973.

Campbell, Joseph. *The Hero with a Thousand Faces.* Meridian Books. Cleveland: World Publishing, 1962.

Davis, Elizabeth Gould. *The First Sex.* New York: G. P. Putnam's Sons,
1971.

Friedan, Betty. *The Feminine Mystique.* New York: W. W. Norton, 1963.

———. *It Changed My Life. Writings on the Women's Movement.* New York:
Random House, 1976.

Harding, M. Esther. *The Way of All Women.* Colophon Books. New York:
Harper & Row, 1975.

———. *Women's Mysteries. Ancient and Modern. A Psychological Interpreta-
tion of the Feminine Principle as Portrayed in Myth, Story, and Dreams.*
New York: G. P. Putnam's Sons, for the C. G. Jung Foundation for
Analytical Psychology, 1971.

Janeway, Elizabeth. *Between Myth and Morning. Women Awakening.* New
York: William Morrow, 1975.

_____. *Man's World, Woman's Place: A Study in Social Mythology.* New York: William Morrow, 1971.

Mead, Margaret. *Culture and Commitment. A Study of the Generation Gap.* Garden City, N.J.: Natural History Press/Doubleday, 1970.

_____. *Male and Female. A Study of the Sexes in a Changing World.* Mentor Book. New York: New American Library, 1955.

Miller, Jean Baker. *Toward a New Psychology of Women.* Boston: Beacon Press, 1976.

Mitchell, Juliet. *Psychoanalysis and Feminism.* New York: Pantheon Books, 1974.

Neumann, Erich. *Amor and Psyche. The Psychic Development of the Feminine.* Translated by Ralph Manheim. Harper Torchbooks/Bollingen Library. New York: Harper & Row, 1962.

_____. *Art and the Creative Unconscious.* Translated by Ralph Manheim. Harper Torchbooks/Bollingen Library. New York. Harper & Row, 1966.

_____. *The Great Mother. An Analysis of the Archetype.* Translated by Ralph Manheim. Bollingen Paperback. Princeton: Princeton University Press, 1974.

_____. *The Origins and Growth of Consciousness.* Two volumes. Translated by R. F. C. Hull. Torchbook edition. New York: Harper & Bros., 1962.

Norman, Dorothy. *The Hero. Myth/Image/Symbol.* An NAL Book. Cleveland: World Publishing Co., 1969.

Richardson, Herbert W. *Nun, Witch, Playmate. The Americanization of Sex.* New York: Harper & Row, 1971.

Sheehy, Gail. *Passages. Predictable Crises of Adult Life.* New York: E. P. Dutton, 1976.

van den Berg, J. H. *The Changing Nature of Mankind. Introduction to a Historical Psychology.* New York: Dell, 1961 (Delta, 1964).

ABOUT THE ME STAGE

Andelin, Helen B. *Fascinating Womanhood.* New York: Bantam, 1975.

Fried, Edrita. *Active/Passive. The Crucial Psychological Dimension.* Colophon edition. New York: Harper & Row, 1971.

Le Shan, Eda. *The Wonderful Crisis of Middle Age.* New York: David McKay, 1973.

Morgan, Marabel. *The Total Woman.* New York: Pocket Books, 1975.

Putney, Snell and Gail. *Normal Neurosis—The Adjusted American.* New York: Harper & Row, 1964.

Steiner, Claude. *Scripts People Live. Transactional Analysis of Life Scripts.* New York: Bantam Books, 1975.

ABOUT THE MYSELF STAGE

Bach, George R., and Goldberg, Herb. *Creative Aggression.* New York: Avon, 1974.

Fensterheim, Herbert, and Baer, Jean. *Don't Say Yes When You Want to Say No.* New York: David McKay, 1975 (Dell Book).

Harris, Thomas A. *I'm OK—You're OK.* New York: Harper & Row, 1969.

James, Muriel, and Jongeward, Dorothy. *Born to Win: Transactional Analysis with Gestalt Experiments.* Reading, Mass.: Addison-Wesley Publishing Co., 1973.

Lynd, Helen Merrell. *On Shame and the Search for Identity.* New York: Science Editions, 1961.

Perls, Frederick S. *Gestalt Therapy Verbatim.* Edited by John S. Stevens. Lafayette, Cal.: Real People Press, 1969.

Smith, Manuel J. *When I Say No, I Feel Guilty.* Bantam Book. New York: Dial Press, 1975

ABOUT THE I STAGE

Erikson, Erik H. *Childhood and Society.* New York: Norton, 1950 (1963).
————. *Insight and Responsibility* New York: Norton, 1964.

Goffman, Erving. *The Presentation of Self in Everyday Life.* Garden City, N.Y.: Doubleday Anchor Books, 1959.

Maslow, Abraham. *Toward a Psychology of Being.* Princeton: Van Nostrand: 1962.

O'Neill, Nena and George. *Shifting Gears. Finding Security in a Changing World.* New York: M. Evans, 1974.

Pogrebin, Letty Cottin. *Getting Yours. How to Make the System Work for the Working Woman.* New York: David McKay, 1975.

Wheelis, Allen. *The Quest for Identity.* New York: Norton, 1958.

ABOUT THE I/THOU STAGE

Becker, Ernest. *The Birth and Death of Meaning.* New York: Free Press of Glencoe, 1962.

_____. *The Denial of Death*. New York: The Free Press, 1973.

_____. *Revolution in Psychiatry*. New York: Free Press of Glencoe, 1964.

Buber, Martin. *I and Thou*. Translated by Ronald Gregor Smith. New York: Scribner's, 1958. (Second edition)

Edinger, Edward F. *Ego and Archetype. Individuation and the Religious Function of the Psyche*. Baltimore: Penguin Books, 1973.

Engelsman, Joan Chamberlain. *The Feminine Dimension of the Divine*. Dissertation. Madison, N.J. Drew University, 1977.

Frankl, Victor. *Man's Search for Meaning. An Introduction to Logotherapy*. New York: Pocket Books, 1963.

Harding, M. Esther. *The "I" and the "Not I." A Study in the Development of Consciousness*. Pantheon Book. New York: Bollingen, 1965.

Kierkegaard, Søren. *The Sickness unto Death*. Garden City, N.Y.: Doubleday Anchor Book, 1954 (published with *Fear and Trembling*).

Singer, June. *Boundaries of the Soul. The Practice of Jung's Psychology*. Garden City, N.Y.: Doubleday Anchor Paperback, 1973.

Tillich, Paul. *The Courage to Be*. Yale Paperbound. New Haven: Yale University Press, 1959.

NOTES

[1]'Abdu'l-Baha, *The Promulgation of Universal Peace*, quoted in Constance Conrader, "Women: Attaining Their Birthright," *World Order*, a Baha'i Magazine, 6 (Summer 1972), p. 55.

[2]H. M. Balyuzi, *Baha'u'llah*, (London: George Ronald, 1963), pp.108–9.

[3]Baha'u'llah, *The Seven Valleys and the Four Valleys* (Wilmette, Illinois: Baha'i Publishing Trust, 1971).